Saving A Life

Vicki-Ann Bush

ALL RIGHTS RESERVED

No part of this book may be reproduced or transmitted in any form or by any means, electronic or mechanical, including photocopying, recording, or by any information storage and retrieval system, without permission in writing from the author, except in the case of brief quotations embodied in reviews.

Publisher's Note:

This is a work of fiction. All names, characters, places, and events are the work of the author's imagination.

Any resemblance to real persons, places, or events is coincidental.

Faccia Brutta Publishing – www.vickiannbush.com

Copyright 2018 –Vicki-Ann Bush • Saving a Life

Second Edition 2020

This book is dedicated to the boy who inspired me to move away from my usual paranormal, young adult fiction and delve into the reality that has taken too many of our children. The boy who captured my heart with a picture, six-year-old Jacob Hall.

On October 1, 2016, Jacob became one of the many children we lost from the horror of school shootings. The innocent face of this little boy continues to take my breath as I remember; he will forever be six years old.

This is for you, Jacob. And although it's like a grain of sand on an endless beach, I will never forget.

"One is loved because one is loved. No reason is needed for loving."

— *Paulo Coelho, The Alchemist*

Chapter One

Walter pulled the comforter down below his chest. His bedroom was beginning to warm as the sun glided through the window. It blanketed his face, soaking up any reminiscence of the almost unbearable chill from the night before. He loved the beauty of winter, but the nights were getting the best of him. At eighty-five, his body was in contention with his mind, and today was one of the harder ones. His legs were stiff and heavy as they dropped off the side of the bed, hitting the floor with as much ease as two fifty-pound barbells. Hello, diabetes.

Missing his slippers, his feet landed on the slick, cold oak floor. Grumbling under his breath about the comforts of carpet, he had to go to the bathroom—pronto. At this point in his life, his teeth were much like his daily memory--there one moment and gone the next. He had pulled them out of the glass of water on the nightstand and thoroughly rinsed them before maneuvering them into his mouth. The mint tickled his palette, and his tongue swirled around inside, pressing them in place. He didn't need them giving into the laws of gravity during breakfast. He never used Polident or any other adhesive; it was messy, and Walter despised anything messy.

He could hear his name being called and opened the bathroom door. *Why must they shout to me every morning? They know I go downstairs promptly at seven o'clock. No mystery, right as clockwork.*

"Yes, Vivienne?"

"Dad, you almost ready? Breakfast is on the table, and it's getting cold. I have to take Robert to pick up his car.

The brakes are finished. I'll only be gone a few minutes."

"Go…go. I'm coming down in a moment. Just need to put on my sweater." *Lovely girl, but a bit daft.* 'I'll be fine."

"Okay. There are eggs and toast. The coffee pot is still on, and your cup is right beside it."

What am I blind now? "Just leave Vivienne. I'm sure I can muster up enough brain power to figure out how to pour a cup of coffee."

He heard the front door close. *Ah, some peace and quiet,* he thought. Walter finished buttoning up his sweater, a dark blue cardigan. His late wife, Gina, gave it to him as a Christmas present…the last Christmas they spent together before she passed away. As he stood head half-cocked looking in the mirror, it reminded him of the first morning he put it on. It was brighter then, and the elbows were not worn like they were now, but it still gave him a feeling of being close to her. A never-ending hug from Gina. As long as he had it, he would always have her arms around him.

He ran his hands down the front, smoothing it out, and then, knees cracking, headed downstairs to the kitchen.

Breakfast was shoveled past his lips. Under-cooked bacon and mediocre eggs slid down with an extra dose of grease.

Pouring a second cup of coffee, he brought it to the front porch to watch the day begin. The front porch was the perfect resting spot to plant himself and observe. As an ex-marine, Walter never forgot his training. He was the unofficial gatekeeper for the block. The snow came unseasonably early this year, and the morning hour left most of the landscape undisturbed. It still had the image of a Thomas Kinkade winter painting. There was something almost magical about the sweeping layers of powdery white, revealing the gleam of a deep freeze. Even neighboring rooftops were transformed from dirty brown shingling to prismatic icicles winking in the sunlight. Each home belonged in a fairy tale you wanted to believe had a happy ending.

Walter's lips almost formed a grin until two cars pulled up in the driveway, and then it was quickly replaced with a scowl. His son, Robert, and wife, Vivienne, were home from the mechanics. As soon as Robert emerged from the driver's seat, Walter rolled his eyes. He knew what was coming.

"It's freezing out here. You're gonna catch pneumonia."

"You can't catch pneumonia from sitting on the porch. Your bum may get a bit chilly, but the threat of pneumonia, I assure you, is not an issue," Walter huffed.

"You know what I mean... What about your arthritis? And don't try to tell me that the cold won't affect it. We both know that's a lie."

"I'm wearing my heavy coat; I have a thermal shirt under my sweater, my old marine boots with wool socks, and a down winter blanket on my legs. I think my arthritis is well protected from the perils of our first snow." Walter slid his hands under the blanket.

"We just worry about you," Robert's eyes narrowed. "Well, since I'm a grown man, and I am the one who raised you, I think you should stop being such a pain in the backside and let me enjoy my peace. And for the love of Henry, tell your wife that I'm not a complete baboon. I know where the kitchen is for breakfast and how to get a cup of coffee. It isn't brain surgery, you know. Although, sometimes, I wonder if the two of you might not benefit from a lobotomy yourselves," Walter looked away.

"That's enough, Dad. Vivienne cooks for you every day. The least you could do is show her a little respect, and a thank you would be nice, too."

Walter pursed his lips, leaned back in his chair, and adjusted the blanket on his legs. "No, son, you're right. I'm sorry, Vivienne. Thank you for breakfast this morning; it was very good."

"You're welcome," Vivienne's eyes brightened with recognition.

"But the next time, could you make my bacon a little crisper. I felt like I was eating a grease-soaked piece of cardboard."

"Dad!"

"No, it's okay, Robert." Vivienne took her husband's hand and squeezed it. "Crisper bacon next time. You got it. Would you like some tea?"

"Thank you, daughter-in-law, that would be fine."

Walter knew what he had said was wrong. But he couldn't help himself. The anger inside just bubbled up; it didn't matter who was in the perimeter of the explosion. They were destined to be one of his many verbal casualties. His sarcasm was sharp and cut like a hunting blade. There were always casualties.

He heard a door slam and turned to his left. The O'Callahan boy, Ryan, was bundled up with a wool pea coat, black leather gloves, and a green plaid scarf wrapped around his face. He was carrying a nylon sports bag on his shoulder. When he reached Walter, he waved and pulled the scarf away from his mouth.

"Good morning, Walter. Isn't it cool outside?"

"Yes, it is cold."

"No, Walter. I meant doesn't everything look really awesome with the snow?" Ryan turned in a circle. Walter chuckled. He knew exactly what Ryan had meant. He was just playing with him. Not wanting to deal with the exhaustion of having to carry on an unwelcome conversation, Walter would often have *trouble understanding people*. This usually led to their frustration and inevitable desire to leave. Mission accomplished. It worked perfectly most of the time. But never with Ryan.

Walter figured the boy was just too dim to realize that his attempt at conversation would continue in an unending loop of sarcasm. Most of the time, he would go into the house and leave Ryan standing outside.

But this morning, he didn't have to. Much to Walter's surprise, he waved one more time and went on his way. *Curious*, thought Walter. *I wonder what that boy is up to?* However, his need to know was short-lived because it wasn't long before he forgot about Ryan O'Callahan and drifted off to sleep.

"Come here, hurry! Come on, you can do it. I'm right here. Reach for my hand, and I'll pull you to me. Don't worry, everything's gonna be okay. I'll take care of you, but you have to come to me. Now!" Walter's body shook violently.

"Dad. Dad! Wake up! You're dreaming," Robert shouted.

Walter slowly opened his eyes. Robert hovered over him with a heavy brow.

"You fell asleep out here. It's been over an hour. Your body is ice cold; we have to get you inside." With a firm grip, he grabbed his father's arm and hoisted him to a standing position.

Walter pushed him away. "I can do it myself. I'm not an invalid, you know. Although the way you and your wife treat me sometimes, you'd think I was ready for the six-foot soil bed."

"You were having one of those dreams, weren't you?" Robert's voice softened.

Walter didn't utter a word. He just shook his head. "Come on, let's get you inside and warm you up. Vivienne made tomato soup and sandwiches for lunch. There's a game going on in a few minutes. We can all watch how badly New England's gonna lose to the Giants."

Walter felt a jolt of excitement liven his weary body. There was nothing he liked more than to watch his favorite football team emerge victoriously. And if they were playing the Patriots, he knew his team wouldn't disappoint him. Before going in, he reached for Robert's arm.

"Son?"

"Yeah?"

"I saw him." Walter's eyes watered.

"I know, Dad. I know you did." Robert patted Walter's back.

Chapter Two

After the Giants' slaughter over the Patriots, Walter felt invigorated. He sat in his cozy recliner and soaked in the victory. Eyeing the room, he noticed that someone, probably Vivienne, had set out a new line of framed photographs in the hutch across the room. One, in particular, caught his attention. It was a photo of Chase, his grandson. He couldn't have been more than four in the picture, and he was standing next to Goofy at Disneyland. His eyes were so bright and his grin so big that it illuminated the photo and diminished the attraction of Sleeping Beauty's castle in the background to a mere color blot.

As the memory flooded his mind, he felt, for a wisp of a second, the happiness of that day. Chase loved Goofy; he was his favorite character. And when they spotted the animated character roaming through the streets of Disneyland greeting the public, Chase ran to him with complete delight. There was no fear or hesitation, just a giant hug when he reached his beloved dog. To see his grandson so filled with joy made every long line and shoving inconsiderate patron just a little inconvenience for Walter. He would do it a thousand times over. And although he'd never admit it to anyone besides Chase, it was his favorite day too. Walter had been a secret Disney fan since the gates parted on July seventeenth, nineteen hundred and fifty-five.

Walter was stationed in southern California after serving in the Korean War. The citrus aroma tickled his nose, drawing him into the endless sun-kissed groves lining the open road. But it was a gentleman named Walt Disney who was about to erupt a volcano of change that would forever impact the sunny state and steal Walter's heart.

The park was honoring military personnel with free admission in celebration of their grand opening. Walter and his buddies invaded Disneyland on the third day of commencement.

Being a strong Marine and admitting to having sentiment for the likes of Cinderella and Snow White left you open for a barrage of unending torment from his veteran friends. Walter quietly cultivated his Disney interest over the years. When he was finally able to share it with his grandson, it was pure nirvana.

Still, in a haze of warm thoughts, another photo caught his eye. This one quickly turned the tides of his memories into a cold abyss. A tear overflowed from the corner of his eye and ran jaggedly down his cheek. Walter quickly swiped it away with the sleeve of his cardigan, cleared his throat, and adjusted his recliner to lay back. The trick was to fool the body. If you imagined every part becoming heavy, starting with the toes and ending with the brain, sleep followed a little easier. Having his mind in an oblivious state was a welcome alternative to the reality of the waking hours lately.

But even with sleep, there wasn't anything to protect him when he was visited by the *dream*. Forget the security of a favorite blanket, the restorative powers of his beloved recliner, or bed; there was no armor against the claws of this particular piece of the subconscious.

Often, deep sleep was met with visions he loved most in life. Memories filled his mind with light, burning the edges of the darkness and cocooning him in a patina of peace. And other times, more specifically, when the light was not strong enough, the darkness took over— bringing that most horrific memory with it. The one that consumed Walter in both reality and dream state. The misery he couldn't and never would be able to let go.

It defined his life in the present and swallowed his desire for any future. As his lids slowly closed and the sounds of the television faded in the distance, he hoped today his dreams would bring him to a place he wanted to be—Disneyland, April twenty-one, two thousand-seven.

Walter woke up to the sound of sirens whizzing past the front of the house. He sat and strained to hear its direction. *When you're on in years and have neighbors who share your decade of life, you tend to pay special attention to where the danger signal is coming from. If the paramedics keep going, you know it's probably not going to be someone you know. It's the volume that winds down near your house that sends fear streaming through your body. Your heart speeds up, and your ears perk up as you head for the window and the pulsing of the glaring lights,* Walter thought.

The song stayed strong and loud as they continued down the block and faded in the distance. Walter let his breath out in a sigh of relief, safe for today.

He lowered his head and spoke a silent prayer for the recipient, something he had learned from his wife, Gina. She would whisper a quick prayer to herself each time she saw an emergency vehicle. She said it was for the folks needing the help, their families, and the ones who were going to their aid. If Walter was the tough muscle of the family, Gina surely was its soft heart. Her kindness and generosity seemed endless to him. He missed her so much, even the smallest routine of having their morning coffee together at the kitchen table left an unfulfilled void.

He pushed forward, and the recliner went to a sitting position. Walter held the arms firmly and slowly put pressure on his legs. Taking in a heavy breath, he stood up and steadied himself. He saw his cane across the room, leaning against the wall, as he cautiously moved toward it. The weight of his legs had been thankfully relieved. Raising them up in the recliner during his nap must have helped his circulation. He opted to avoid the cane and head to the kitchen—something smelled delicious.

The closer he got, the stronger the scent permeated through the hallway. Meatloaf ... his favorite.

Although he would never tell Vivienne, she made a meatloaf nearly as tantalizing as Gina's, which was a lot for Walter to say about a German. Gina had been of Italian descent; Vivienne was not. Her *people* were half German and half English. A disaster for food where he was concerned. He loved the homemade lasagna, manicotti, meatballs, and other pasta dishes that Gina took all day to prepare. Sunday was always gravy day. That's what her family called tomato sauce. And although Walter was of full Irish descent, he had blended into the ways of Gina's family with complete bliss—for the food.

Vivienne stood at the kitchen stove with her back to him. She hadn't heard him come in and he stood privately admiring her. She was a lot like Gina when it came to family. It was so easy for her to take care of everyone, rarely focusing on herself. He often gave her such a hard time; he didn't know why he did that. *Why couldn't he tell her that he loved her like a daughter?* She was the best thing in his son's life, and yet, all he threw at her were insults and indignation.

How could she even lift her head off the pillow? And yet, there she was, cooking dinner for him and Robert, managing to put one foot in front of the next and functioning. She had such strength ... she didn't deserve his wrath. It wasn't her fault, none of it. It was all his.

"Something smells mighty good." Walter took a seat at the kitchen table. Vivienne spun around and, without hesitation, wiped her hands on her apron and cut a piece of Italian bread that was on a cutting board on the counter. She neatly layered butter on the top and set it down next to Walter.

"Thank you. Is that your meatloaf in the oven?" Walter took a bite of bread.

"Yes, and it's almost done. So, no more bread Dad, until dinner. I made mashed potatoes and peas too. I don't want you full before we even sit down to eat. How was your nap? Peaceful?" Vivienne had her back to him.

He knew what she was getting at, but he wasn't going to take the bait. She didn't need to go down this road again. "Yes, it was quite nice. I feel much better. The sirens woke me, though. Did you hear them?"

"I did. I was listening to the radio, and they said there was a major accident on Third and Florence. I guess there were four or five cars involved. There's already one fatality. Those poor people. It's so cold out, too, that makes the condition so much worse. I wonder if it was ice?"

"If what was ice?" Walter knitted his brows. He hated when they went off point. It was so damn confusing.

"The accident. I wonder if ice on the road was to blame. It's been pretty slippery out there. I told Robert they really need to drive slower during this weather."

"I heard my name. What did you tell me?" Robert came strolling in and went straight to the bread. Vivienne grabbed the cutting board and handed him one slice. He opened his mouth to argue, but she quickly put her hand up. He decided to heed the warning—her meatloaf was too good to pass up.

He grabbed the butter and sat across from Walter at the table. "What were you two talking about? And how does it involve me?"

"It doesn't," Walter was gruff. "Vivienne was just saying that it's slippery outside."

"Well, I see you're in rare form tonight, Dad. I'm in a good mood, so I'll choose to ignore that." He finished buttering his bread and took a large bite. "Viv, do you think you could do without me for a few hours tomorrow night? Jim called and asked if I'd help him with the new DVD player and TV he bought. You know how frustrated he gets with electronics."

"I'll try to weather through." She put her hands over her heart and smirked.

"I know you're heartbroken, but it will save us time in the long run.

If I let him attempt to set them up on his own, he'll just succeed in screwing it up so badly it will take me half the day to undo what he has done. You know I'm right; after all, he's your brother."

Vivienne stuck her tongue out at him and proceeded to turn around and finish the mashed potatoes.

"What about you, Dad? Would you like to join me tomorrow night at Jim's house? It's been a while since you've been over there. I know the kids would love to see you." Jim and his wife, Samantha, had two children. Sadie, who was four, and Derek, seven.

"I don't think so. I'm not feeling very well. I think it's the cold; it's making all my muscles ache."

"Oh, come on. I know what you're doing. You have to see Jim some time. You can't cut him out of the rest of your life. Eventually, you won't be able to avoid it."

"I said no. Now leave me alone, and let me enjoy my last bite of bread." Walter tucked the last morsel in his mouth and leaned back into his chair. He closed his eyes and enjoyed the saltiness of the creamy butter on the warm Italian bread. It was so fresh. Another Gina memory.

When they were very young, they practically survived on Italian bread from the bakery. It was cheap and filling. He felt a lump form in his throat. Quickly he rose and went to the bathroom… he mustn't let them see him cry.

He could hear Vivienne's voice carrying down the hallway. She was muttering something about not going too far because dinner was about done. He closed the door and leaded into it. He stood in the bathroom and sobbed like a child.

He caught a glance at himself in the mirror and then reached for a wad of toilet paper. Blowing his nose and then splashing cold water on his face, he returned to the kitchen.

Vivienne was placing the plates of food on the table, and Robert stood at the counter pouring drinks. Merlot wine for Vivienne, Jack Daniels and Coke for Robert, and for Walter, iced tea. Walter never cared much for liquor and couldn't fathom water by itself, so Vivienne persuaded him to try the chilled version of black tea. He rather enjoyed it when sweetened with Equal and loaded with lemon slices. Since he was a diabetic, it was a shot of insulin before dinner to steady the sugars from rising to Defcon five. Walter could not forgo this ritual at the dinner table as he had done that morning. Nope. He was now under the hawk-like, watchful eye of his daughter-in-law. With complete focus, she would stand and wait. Observing his every move until the pen penetrated his skin, releasing the lifesaving serum. Done.

Dinner was comfortably quiet until Robert decided to ruin it.

"Dad. Ryan stopped by earlier when you were napping. It seems there is a new program at the Frontier Park Community Center.

Swimming classes and water aerobics for seniors in the neighborhood. He thought you might be interested. I guess a real crowd signed up. It might be good for your diabetes." Robert placed his elbow on the table and, resting his cheek on his hand, leaned into Walter. "What do you say? Swimming, friends, some time away from us? That alone should be your incentive, I would think.

Besides, I heard Lillian will be there. You've always enjoyed mulling over the past with her. Could be a good thing."

"It's freezing outside, and you want me to get into a pool? Now I know you've lost your last brain cell." Walter shook his head and then shot a look straight to Vivienne. "Are you in on this too? You want me out of the house? What, am I too much in the way? Do you have some sort of plans you don't want me to see?" Walter's words dripped with venom.

"Enough!" Robert's face flushed red with anger. "Why must you continue this? I honestly don't understand why Viv doesn't just..."

Vivienne grabbed his arm, and Robert stopped.

"No, it's not that I want you out of the house. It's just that I… we want you to start talking with people again. It's been over a year now. And no one knows more than us how difficult this is. But you're slipping away; we see it, and, quite frankly, we're not ready for you to go anywhere just yet. Besides, the pool is indoors." Vivienne pushed the pamphlet across the table.

"Fourteen months, sixteen days." Walter scanned for the clock on the kitchen wall. "And nine hours."

Robert and Vivienne exchanged the same sadness in their eyes as they heard the words ring through the air.

They both knew precisely what Walter was referring to, but neither one could give it any life. Instead, Robert picked up the pamphlet and leafed through it before setting it back down beside Walters's plate.

"Just look at it, Dad. The pool is inside and heated. It might do your arthritis good and help with regulating your diabetes if you get some exercise." Robert's gaze took his line of sight up to the ceiling. He calmed his breath and then met Walter's eyes. "We were only thinking of you. Whatever you decide is up to you. We won't bring it up again."

Walter picked up the pamphlet, read the first page, and then tossed it into the nearby trash. The three of them finished their dinner without another word.

Chapter Three

Walter heard a loud explosion of bullets. They were coming so fast he couldn't think. He reached out and then dove to the ground. "Come here! I can help you, but you have to get to me first. Please, listen to what I'm saying. It's going to be alright. You can do it. I know it's loud; concentrate on my voice. Just hear me; come to me. Now … now!" Walter shot up to a sitting position. He strained to focus his eyes in the darkness. A tall dresser, coat rack … he was in his bedroom. His pajamas were soaked through with sweat, and he started to shiver. The room was cold. The first thought to run through his mind was to get up and change, but exhaustion gripped his body. He pulled the comforter up to his neck and lay back down. Turning to his side and praying for peace, he drifted back to sleep.

By the time Walter opened his eyes again, the light of the morning sun was streaming through his room. He scouted around his surroundings, searching for his robe. Vivienne had Chase pick it out for him two Christmases ago. Chase was so excited to give it to him that he practically tore all the wrapping paper off before Walter could get his hands on it. Dark blue, Walter's favorite color. *Ah, there it is.* He spotted it lying over the back of his chair in the corner next to his reading table. Slowly he got up. His knees and ankles creaked, and Walter laughed to himself. When he was in the service, many times their mission required a level of silence that he had perfected with complete precision. But there wouldn't be any sneaking up on anyone any longer. He stood for a moment admiring his grandson's gift and basking in the memory. Running his hands across the fabric, it was warm from the sunlight that had melted over it.

Another trip down the staircase meant more creaking and popping. He really should have bought a one-story.

After a breakfast of Cream of Wheat and orange juice, Walter poured a hot cup of black coffee and went out to sit on the porch. He didn't bother with a coat. Fastening the belt on his robe and flipping up the collar would be a sufficient barrier from the icy cold. He was wrong. After five minutes of nestling into his favorite bench on the porch, he went back in for his coat.

"Tell me you didn't just go out there in only your robe." Vivienne stood with her arms crossed.

Her lips were pressed so tightly together that it made Walter laugh to himself. They almost looked like they were glued shut. *Clearly, she was perturbed.* "I did but only for a few minutes. I came back in for my coat."

"You're gonna get sick doing things like that. You need to be more careful. Have you taken your insulin this morning?"

"Pfff…It's fine. I'll take it tonight." Walter batted his hand in the air.

"You know this is not an option. This is the second morning you haven't had it. You can't just decide when or when not to take it. The doctor told you this is something you must be consistent with. If Robert knew, he'd have a fit."

"If Robert knew?" Walter was offended and getting angry. "Let me tell you something, little miss. I am Robert's father, not the other way around. I do not need a nursemaid, and I certainly do not need to answer to my son. If anything is going to kill me, it will be the two of you raising my blood pressure. Now get the heck off my back and leave me alone. I will be out front sitting on the porch. I would prefer to do this on my own.

"Do not ask me if I need anything, do not follow me out babbling the same needlessly petty conversation I hear nearly every day of my life. I want peace and quiet. Are you capable of that? Don't bother to answer; just shake your head."

Vivienne stiffened her tiny five-foot-two-inch frame. Her hands clenched tightly in a fist, she bit her bottom lip and took a deep breath. Walter knew he had pushed her to her limits. And yet, she just turned away and walked into the kitchen without acknowledging the wounds his sharp tongue inflicted. He hurt her repeatedly when she was already consumed with it on her own. He said nothing more and stepped out to the porch.

Walter settled back into his cushioned bench and relaxed. Portions of the snow had already begun to melt on the pavement. It looked slushy, like those drinks the kids love from Seven-Eleven. This slush wasn't an electric blue or pink cotton candy but a murky gray from the mixture of dirt, tainting the picture-perfect land of enchantment from just twenty-four hours ago. His eyes explored each side of the street. First to the right and then to the left. Nothing. No one was out and about. Either it was too cold or too early. Either way, Walter preferred it that way. Just the serene morning air. And then *he* came out.

"Hi, Walter. It's pretty cold today. Aren't you freezing?" Ryan kept walking toward Walter, up the pathway, and finally stopping at the base of the porch.

Walter shook his head and looked away. He didn't utter a word. *How dare he interrupt my peaceful morning!* He thought. *I never invited him to come over, and yet here he stands. The kids today are disrespectful, lazy, and assuming. They think the world owes them. Nothing ... that is what they are owed,* "In my day, children had respect for their elders. I did not invite you to come over, so why are you here?"

Ryan wasn't easily riled. He had known Walter nearly all his life. He knew that Walter used to be a happy, patient guy. He remembered when he was younger, he'd spend most of his summers on the porch listening to Walter's old war stories. They were so interesting, and Walter never minded spending time with him. But all that had changed, and Ryan understood why. So, he stood his ground and politely answered. "Sorry I disturbed you, Walter. I'm actually here to talk to Robert. Is he home?"

Walter simply pointed to the front door and remained gazing down the block. Ryan knocked, and in a few moments, Vivienne appeared with a smile. She invited Ryan in, never once saying anything to Walter. After their last conversation, Walter figured she knew it was better to leave him be.

Vivienne led Ryan into the kitchen and yelled upstairs for Robert to come down. She pulled a chair out for Ryan to be seated. Placing a few cookies on a plate, she then put a kettle of water on the stove to boil for hot chocolate. "How's your Mom and Dad? And Grace?" Vivienne grinned to herself.

Grace was Ryan's girlfriend, and although he hadn't admitted it to them, it was clear when they were together. They were the cutest couple. She still remembered the day he brought her by to introduce her to Walter and the family. He and Walter had been so close at one time. Grace was shy and polite, with a posture of strength and quiet confidence. Vivienne liked her instantly.

"Mom and Dad are actually away visiting my uncle in California. Dad keeps calling and taunting me with the temperature out there. It's cruel." He smirked. "I told him I'm gonna leave all the snow for him to shovel when he gets home.

Somehow I know he didn't believe me." When Robert came in, Ryan and Vivienne were laughing at the prospect of his house having snow piled up to the roof.

"Hey Ryan, what's going on? Did you need me?" Robert snatched a few of the cookies, and Vivienne slapped his hand.

"Those are for Ryan. Besides, you've had your cookie quota for the day."

"Okay, but you know that's really not fair. You know how much I love your baking."

Vivienne rubbed his belly. "Uh, I think sometimes, maybe a little too much."

"Hey!" Robert sat down at the table and pushed the plate of cookies closer to Ryan.

"And Grace?" Vivienne sat down.

"Grace is doing great." Ryan blushed. "That's actually what I wanted to talk to you about, Robert. I'm glad you're home too, Vivienne. It's about Walter. Grace has started working with the program down at the pool. Honestly, I really do think it might be a good thing for Walter. I dropped the pamphlet off to you earlier, Robert, remember?"

"Ah, yeah. And I did show it to Walter. He, in turn, threw it in the trash. I saw it when I went to pull out the garbage bag. To say this is an impossible sell would be a very large understatement, Ryan. And Vivienne and I did discuss it. We thought it would be a wonderful idea. But actually, getting Walter to agree and then go … we are swimming against the tide, kid."

"I know he's stubborn; I do. But will you guys give me a crack at him? Maybe I can be more persuasive."

Ryan leaned into the plate of cookies, surveying them for the one that looked the most appealing.

"Besides, I don't live with him. If he growls at me, I go home. On the other hand, you two have to hear him for the rest of the day."

Robert pursed his lips, widened his eyes, and nodded his head in agreement. Then he turned to Vivienne. "What do you think, beautiful? Should we throw Ryan to the lions?"

She rolled her eyes and nodded in agreement.

"Okay, kid, you're up. But don't expect much. In fact, don't expect anything. And if I were you, I'd grab a shield, maybe some armor while you're at it. Viv, do you still have that sword we picked up at the Renaissance Fair? I mean, poor Ryan can't go unarmed."

Ryan was chewing a cookie and snorted and laughed so hard, a piece shot out onto the table. "I think I can handle this, Robert."

He took a sip of the hot chocolate and grabbed one more cookie. Thanking Vivienne, he headed out to the porch and the inaccessible Walter.

Walter heard the squeak of the door as it opened. He looked over his shoulder and saw Ryan emerge. Once again, he turned away. He liked the boy; he really did. But talking with Ryan was too painful.

It reminded him of times he would never have and a past that would always be better than anything the future could bring. He hoped he would just leave and not try to engage him in conversation. But he didn't get his wish.

Ryan sat down on the other end of the bench.

Walter flipped up the collar of his coat, tightened his body, and, drawing his legs in from their previous sprawl, crossed his arms tightly across his chest. He was now an impenetrable force.

Ryan waited a full minute before attempting to speak.

"Walter, do you remember Lillian Granger? Ryan leaned in closer.

"Well, it's a shame what has been going on with her lately. Yeah, I'm pretty worried. Not sure if she's going to come out of this. I mean,

I know she's ninety-two, but I thought we'd have her around for a few more years. Grace told me she was worried too. You remember Grace, right Walter? She's participating in the senior pool classes with me. She is a great lifeguard."

Walter squirmed a little. He wanted so badly to ask Ryan what was wrong with Lillian. She was a favorite of his. When Gina passed away, Lillian came every day to bring him food and just sit on the porch with him. She's a good woman, he thought. He couldn't hold his tongue any longer. "What's wrong with her?"

"Oh, so you do remember her?" Ryan said coyly.

"Of course, I do. I'm old, not brain-dead, boy." Walter huffed.

"She was hit hard with a severe case of arthritis.

That's why she's at the pool. The doctor is hoping some water activity will help her. It's so sad; she can barely walk. Her daughter brings her five days a week. I'm not sure if it's going to work, though."

"Why wouldn't it? Isn't water very good for arthritis?" Walter twisted in his seat.

"It is. But she's in so much pain. I'm afraid it's pushed her down into a deep depression. Remember how lively and talkative she used to be? No more. Most of the time, she just sits like a stone staring off into nowhere. That's one of the reasons I asked you to come. Maybe an old friend is just what she needs to lighten her spirit. I mean, it's worth a shot, isn't it?" Ryan looked directly into Walter's eyes.

He knew the kid was playing on his emotions. *Damn—it worked. How could he cast off Lillian without trying to help her? After everything she had done for him, she was such a good friend. Now it was his turn, even if it meant doing something that made him want to scream inside. Just the thought of spending several hours a day with this kid, his pixie girlfriend, and a bunch of yapping old fossils gave him a sharp pain in his head. For sure, his ears would bleed at some point from all the pointless droning. But, he must go—for Lillian.*

"Walter, you see my dilemma. I'm really concerned. Do you think you might reconsider? Maybe come a couple of days a week, just for a few hours. It would mean a lot to her, I know it."

"Stop, kid. I know what you're trying to do. Is she really in a bad way?"

"She is."

"I'll come." Walter released his arms and rested his hands on his thighs. The ambush was over.

"That's great, I'll—."

"You'll nothing. I'll have my daughter-in-law drop me off tomorrow. You can give her all the details. Now go home." Walter turned away—their discussion had ended.

Ryan went back into the house to give Robert the information. He emerged with a smile so wide, the gleam needed its own SPF.

With taught lips and a wrinkled brow, Walter watched as Ryan leaped off the porch and dashed home. Snow began to fall, and the cold was chilling him to shivers. It was time to go in. As usual, he entered the living room, took off his coat, and hung it on one of the brass hooks fastened to the wall by the front door. Pivoting toward the dining room, the picture he had spotted on the hutch earlier seemed to call out to him. It was enough to stop him and make him shake. How could Vivienne put that damn thing out? It did no good for anyone. As he scanned all the little smiling faces, he found Chasey.

His brown hair was messy, and he wore his favorite Batman shirt. Walter remembered the tug-of-war Vivienne had with him that morning and, for a moment, the tears halted, and a smile emerged. It was class picture day, and Chase was adamant about wearing that t-shirt. Vivienne, of course, wanted him to put on something that was, well, not superhero. Chase won. He'd stood tall and proud for his photo. Walter trudged over to the picture and picked it up. Chuckling, he noticed not only did Chase have on his Batman t-shirt but his watch, as well.

That boy, he whispered to himself, strong-headed like his Grandma. Walter felt a rush of pain in his chest and his knees weaken. His unsupported legs buckled beneath him. He dropped the picture and started sobbing uncontrollably.

Vivienne and Robert were still in the kitchen and rushed in. Vivienne saw the photo and immediately knew what had happened. "I'm sorry, Dad. I shouldn't have put it out. But he looked so happy. Mrs. Harper had dropped it off a few weeks ago, and I finally found a frame I liked. I'll put it in our bedroom." She swiftly turned the photo over and helped Robert lift Walter and bring him over to his recliner. "No. Keep it out." Walter laid his head back on the recliner and pushed with his body, raising his feet.

"It's okay, you're right. He looks happy. Leave it." He shut his eyes and pretended to drift off to sleep. He had hoped this would be enough for them to leave him alone with his thoughts.

Vivienne gently placed the picture back on the hutch and adjusted it a few times before grabbing Robert's hand and squeezing it. His face was limp with sadness, and she could see by the water filling his eyes that he was fighting off the tears that wanted to break free. She squeezed his hand again and nodded toward the kitchen. He let her lead him, and Walter was, once again, alone.

Chapter Four

Several days went by before Walter got the word from Robert that Vivienne would be dropping him off at the pool in the morning. He had hoped that the conversation with Ryan was one of his many vivid dreams, but to his disappointment, it was most definitely his reality. It was his last day of freedom before his sentence at the pool was set to begin, and a television marathon was his last supper. Walter liked sitting in front of the fantasy box, his private name for television. Westerns, shoot 'em ups, and, oh yes, Dirty Harry movies. Walter was a huge Clint Eastwood fan and had been since the early days of his spaghetti westerns. A term that was penned for western films made in Italy. Walter always thought that was a funny thing. A western made in a country that didn't have cowboys. He didn't mind, though; he loved them.

The morning started with old episodes of Bonanza, a show that Walter never grew tired of. He had probably watched each one fifty times, but it didn't matter. The good movies didn't come on until after lunch, so he was content to spend some quality time with his television family, Ben, little Joe, Adam, and Hoss.

Settling back in his recliner, he draped his small blanket over his legs. The cold bothered him more than usual the past few weeks, and the thought of getting in the pool tomorrow gave him the shivers. But at least he was content for today.

Vivienne had made a plate of sliced apples and set it on a tray beside the recliner before dashing out to meet with friends. Walter had the house to himself, and he couldn't be happier. It had been a while since Vivienne had made time to spend with her friends.

He let his eyes wander to the picture on the hutch. Chasey's smile was full, like two red apples for cheeks. Walter couldn't help but smile in return. Chasey's grin was infectious. But then the memories, the grim reaper of happiness, rushed in and took with them the minute of joy he had felt. All that was left was the overwhelming and suffocating reality. Quickly he averted his eyes toward the television and concentrated on the perils of the Cartwright's latest danger.

He was halfway through the third episode when he heard sirens. Walter quickly paused the picture and waited. As they got louder, he mumbled a prayer to himself. But this time, they didn't keep going. He listened for the *woot, woot* sound the paramedic's truck made when approaching its destination. It was only a few doors down. *Oh no*, he thought, *who now?* He pushed the recliner down and slowly got to his feet. His cane was hooked on the tray table, and he clutched it with his right hand. Steadying himself, he shuffled to the window. The lights were bright against the gray day and the stark white snow. They stopped in front of a little brown house across the street and two over to Walter's left. He could see them navigating the path with their bags in hand. One of the paramedics slipped and nearly took a spill, but he managed to secure his footing and avert going down. "Damn," Walter cursed. "Not the Taylors."

Grabbing his coat from the hook, he bundled up and carefully stepped out onto the porch. He couldn't see anyone, so he decided to get closer. The steps had iced over, and even though Robert had layered them with sand, he knew they could be dangerous. Slowly he took the steps one at a time until reaching the bottom. The city cleared the streets, but the sidewalks were the homeowners' responsibility. His son was diligent in keeping them clear, but not everyone shared Robert's zealous nature.

Walter assessed the best route to take with the least amount of snow and decided to cross the street right in front of his house. Vincent Dalo had just finished salting to create a safer path.

Looking both ways, he ventured across. As he approached the other side, Vincent was waiting in front of his home.

"Walter. Careful. It's still a slip hazard. Do you know what's happening?" Vincent's voice could carry over a stadium filled with Yankee fans.

Walter shook his head back and forth. "I'm not sure if they are there for Frank or Elsa."

"I think it might be Elsa. I spoke to Frank yesterday, and he said she wasn't feeling well. Flu-like symptoms and severe coughing. He wanted to take her to the doctor, but you know Elsa, as stubborn as she is beautiful."

Elsa was beautiful. Even at seventy-two, she could turn heads. Five feet-eight, slender, and a profile that belonged on a magazine cover from the golden age of glamour. She could melt a camera lens with envy. Her hair was as blonde as the deepest golden wheat, naturally at one time, but now the beauty parlor kept that brilliance for her. Walter always had a fondness for Elsa. Gina was the love of his life, but Elsa was like a schoolboy crush. And one he would never think to reveal. The two men waited until the front door flew open, and they and a gurney emerged. Frank was following behind and caught sight of them.

"It's Elsa! She's stopped breathing! Oh, please pray for her. We're on our way to Bethlehem Memorial," Frank was still talking as one of the paramedics helped him in the back of the vehicle as they prepared to drive away.

Walter stood fixated on the shrinking image as yet another friend might make what seemed all too common lately—the one-way journey.

27 Saving a Life

"I'm going to head over to the hospital. Do you want to come with me, Walter?" Vincent hobbled toward his car.

Walter wanted to go. He wanted to be there for his friends, but to the hospital? No, he just couldn't do it. Too many bad memories, too much death. "No. I'll wait here and tell Vivienne. Will you call me and let me know what's happening?"

"Sure." Vincent got in his car and drove away.

Walter surveyed the vehicle as the melting snow sloshed under the tires and flung itself out to the middle of the street and the side of the road. It just looked so dirty. No longer peaceful and white, just stale and tainted. He made his way back inside, took off his coat, and plopped back down in his chair. He was exhausted. It was long before his body surrendered.

"Dad. Wake up." Walter could feel the sweat trickling down his forehead and taste the saltiness as it reached his tongue. The back of his collar was soaked through. It stuck to his neck, sending chills down his spine. As he was being jostled abruptly, he heard his son say, "Dad."

"Stop shaking me," Walter snapped.

"I'm sorry, but you were dreaming again. I tried calling to wake you, but I couldn't. You were yelling his name again. Over and over. I'm sorry, but I couldn't hear it any longer." The corners of Vivienne's mouth drooped.

Walter didn't say a word. Nothing he could offer would help; he knew it. She didn't need to be reminded further.

He reached up and patted the back of her hand resting on his shoulder. She nodded and went upstairs. His dreams were so vivid, so real. He longed for the day they would fade, and yet, the same thought left him riddled with fear. It was his only connection to *him*.

The only time he still felt real. Walter consciously switched his concentration back to the fantasy box and happy endings.

The sun set, and not long after, Robert came barreling through the door. His coat was covered in a layer of snow, and Walter could only assume it had begun to come down again—hard.

"Burr, it's freezing out there. I can't believe how cold I got just going from the car to the house. I think we're going to have another record storm. The sky is eerie, and the snow is falling fast. I could barely see driving the last few blocks. I hope Viv cooked up something really hardy, like a stew. I need to warm my bones. I think I'll start with a bourbon. How was your day?"

"Okay. They took Elsa away by paramedics today," Walter answered in a monotone.

"Oh jeez, no. Did it look very serious?" Robert reached for his drink and sat down on the couch.

"Yeah. It was very serious—she stopped breathing. Frank was a raving lunatic. He rode over with her in the back with the paramedics. Vincent followed with his car. I thought it best I stay behind, and this way, I could tell you and Viv what was going on."

He nodded in agreement. "I think that was a good idea. Do you know which hospital they took her to?"

"Bethlehem Memorial. I've been waiting, thinking Vincent would call, but I haven't heard anything."

"I'll call the hospital after dinner. Give them a little more time to do their job. Okay?"

"I guess so." Walter wanted to thank his son properly, but something always made him hold back. It didn't use to be this way with Robert. When he was a boy, they were so close. But since that day, the one that changed everything, he couldn't seem to let anyone break his hardened shell. It was easier that way.

Robert took a quick sip from his drink and then mumbled he was going upstairs to change into sweats. Slowly and with a plethora of cracking bones, Walter rose from his chair and hobbled across the room to the front window. The snow was so thick he could barely see the houses across the street, but he had enough visibility to see Vincent hadn't gotten back home yet. The twinkling diamonds floating on the surface of the puffy freeze brought peace. Even the descending snow added to the calm. Walter sighed.

He leaned his forehead on the window and closed his eyes. The cold seeped through his skin, giving him a searing pain, but he didn't move. As great as the chill hurt, it brought with it a memory. His last winter with Chasey and the coldest day in twenty years.

Robert and Vivienne had gone into the city early that morning. It was their anniversary, and Robert had surprised her with a night of romance and a suite at the poshest hotel money could buy. Walter had promised Chasey that they would embark on their own adventure, and the boy was jumping with excitement. To begin, they would do breakfast at the diner, then a stroll in the park for sledding, an afternoon movie with lots of popcorn, and lastly, a trip to T&R Toys on the way home.

They had the perfect day planned. Until the freeze came. About mid-morning, right after breakfast, a severe cold front whipped through their town and took with it all of the day's plans. Streets and sidewalks were laden with ice. Public transportation had halted, and the snow alternated with large chunks of hail.

Walter barely made it home with Chasey before the forty-mile-an-hour winds decided to add to the destruction. Chasey was devastated. He moped around, flopping down on the couch and even refusing to play with his video games. Desperate, Grandpa Walter decided to take a day from his childhood.

Chasey watched as he went from closet to closet, stealing the treasure of pillows and clothes pins, amassing all the blankets and sheets he could find in the house, and ending in the dining room. Boxes of cookies, chocolate milk cartons, and potato chips completed the foundation for paradise.

Curiosity burned through Chasey's bad mood. He got up and went into the dining room. Walter had constructed the most enormous blanket tent the boy had ever seen. He even put his little battery-operated train set in the center of it. There were coloring books, action figures, and some of his favorite books. Chasey ran over to investigate. Walter lifted the flap and invited his grandson to join him. It was like being in another world, one just for them. A secret place where anything was possible. Walter told him stories about his childhood, the war, and Robert at his age. Chasey loved it. They stayed all day and night in their special world, where action figures watched over their dreams and grandpas ruled the universe.

It was Walter's fondest memory and most painful one. They were so happy that day. A time for magic and adventure.

He thought he would have many more of those days with his grandson. If he had only known, maybe he could have made it even better, tried harder. The darkness started creeping into his mind once again, like a deadly fungus killing off all that was good and leaving a shell of emptiness. He was succumbing once again.

"Dinner," He heard Vivienne calling from the kitchen. Like a rubber band tightly stretched and quickly released, Walter snapped back. He pulled away from the window rubbing his hand on his chilled forehead to warm it. Clearing his throat and wiping the moisture off his cheeks, he prepared himself for dinner and the uninviting conversation that came along with it.

"Listen to me. We *are* going to get home today. Just do as I say, and it will be okay. Don't look back; just come to me. Quickly, run. It's alright. I know you're scared. I'm here with you, but you have to listen. Come now … *now*! Chasey!" Walter woke to uncontrollable shivers and a sharp pain in his chest. Today was his first day for the unwanted new social hell he agreed to endure. It couldn't be worse than his dreams, though, and that thought gave him the strength to rise out of bed.

He wanted to catch Robert before he left for work, so he opted to throw on his robe instead of dressing. They had been waiting all night to hear from Vincent regarding Elsa. When Robert called earlier in the evening, Vincent told him he would stay at the hospital with Frank so he wouldn't be alone. He promised to call as soon as there was some news. Walter waited up until nearly midnight, which was hours past his usual ten o'clock turn-in time. But the phone remained stubbornly silent.

He took the stairs quicker than usual but kept a firm grip on the rail. He didn't need a trip to the hospital himself. Although maybe he and Elsa could be room buddies. He hated the thought of such a lovely woman sharing a room with strangers. He knew she definitely didn't have the luxury of a room to herself. Medicare would never pay for that. No way. It was the buddy system for anyone their age on a fixed income. As he reached the last step, he caught Robert heading out the door.

"Morning Dad. I'm in a hurry, woke up late this morning. The damn alarm didn't go off. I think it's broken. Vivienne has breakfast warming in the oven for you. She's in the shower getting ready to take you to class today. Enjoy it, and try not to stir things up on your first day." Robert tilted his head to the right and flashed a brief smile.

"Wait!" Walter nearly slipped.

"I'm really in a hurry. Vivienne will be done soon. Whatever it is, she can help you."

"No. I don't need help. For heaven's sake, I'm your father. Give me a minute of your precious time."

Robert adjusted his shoulders and put himself in check. None of them were very patient anymore. "Sorry. What is it?"

"I just want to know if you heard anything from Vincent or Frank about Elsa?"

"No, we haven't. But Vivienne said she would stop by the hospital after she dropped you off. You should know something after your class."

Walter grumbled under his breath as Robert hastily whisked through the doorway, slamming the front door.

The kitchen had a familiar aroma, one of Walter's favorites. He could almost taste the cinnamon and apples as he opened the oven door and saw Vivienne's homemade pancakes. Adding to the yum, was fresh apple compote that drizzled over the top and ran down the sides. On the table sat a can of whipped cream and a place setting for one with his empty coffee cup. Walter quickly grabbed the two potholders beside the stove and placed the pan with his delectable breakfast on the burners.

Grabbing a spatula from the drawer, he slid his pancakes neatly on his plate and loaded up the whipped cream. Pouring his coffee, he added nothing, preferring it black. In fact, he could never understand why someone would want to ruin a good cup of Joe with sugar or milk. It seemed a pointless addition to an already perfect blend of flavor.

Savoring the decadent mix of breakfast and dessert, Walter allowed the flavors to cancel out the memory of yesterday's disappointing menu option.

He cleaned his plate of the last bite and placed the dish in the sink. Vivienne preferred to load the dishwasher herself. Walter knew better than to argue with a woman about her kitchen. He went upstairs to shower and dress for the drive down the green mile, a comparison that Walter had made in his mind and one he felt confident describing his little outing for the day.

It was still extremely cold out so in addition to packing his bathing suit and towel, he placed an extra sweatshirt in his bag. There was no way he was about to shower at the facility. God knows what germs lurked amidst the damp, dark corners.

Walter sat on his bed for a moment feeling the warmth of the sunlight streaming in. This could be a normal day, a good day, he hoped. There really weren't any more of those left for him and getting in a pool wouldn't bring them back. However, he gave his word to Ryan, and he never went back on his word. Putting pressure on his legs to stand, he noticed they felt heavier, stiffer. He shuffled instead of picking up his feet, which seemed to help.

Vivienne was waiting all buttoned up with scarf and hat in place. When she saw Walter, her face lit up. The porch was still covered with snow, and they both took their time going down the stairs. The cold stung Walter's face like tiny jabbing needles. He flipped the collar of his coat up to better protect the back of his neck from suffering the same fate. Walter thought he should thank her for such a delicious breakfast, but the words wouldn't come. He found himself gazing out the window in silence. After several blocks of houses whisking by, he turned and took in the vision of his daughter-in-law. She had her scarf wrapped around her jaw and mouth, leaving only the upper portion of her face exposed. He had always thought she had the most stunning pale blue eyes, and with the glare of the sunlight shining on them, they were almost transparent. Chasey had the same pale blue eyes. Walter quickly looked away.

He needed to stay in the moment today. He didn't notice the speed bump as the car nearly halted and gently climbed over it. He was too busy staring at the large beige building—they had arrived.

Chapter Five

After much insistence, Walter left Vivienne in the car and went in on his own. The first thing he saw when entering was a counter about four feet high and crescent-shaped. Standing behind it were two young employees. Walter estimated they were no older than sixteen or seventeen. *Great*, he thought, *I'm surrounded by the lollipop guild.* Behind them, mounted on the wall, was a large chalkboard. It had the water temperature, the classes for the day, and which swimming lanes were open. Walter was about to ask how to get into the pool area when he saw Ryan emerge through two double doors on the opposite side of the room. As they slowly closed, he got a glimpse of the pool. Usually confident and relatively not rattled by most of the happenings in his day-to-day, Walter's stomach felt queasy. He was nervous, and he didn't have a clue why.

"Walter, you're here!" Ryan exclaimed. "I'm so glad you came. Come on, I'll show you where to change, and we'll pick out a locker to put your bag in. The water is heated, so don't worry about the cold in here. I don't know if you noticed, but the board has the last reading at 80 degrees. Nice and warm."

Walter nodded. He couldn't get over the growing feeling that captured the pit of his stomach and was holding his usual confidence prisoner. He clutched his bag closer to his body like a security blanket for a toddler.

Ryan got him settled, showed him the door to exit to the pool area, and then left him to his privacy. Walter thought about making a run for it, but the freezing temperature and lack of transportation made that idea null and void. The smell of chlorine and wetsuits carried him back to the many times he and Gina spent their summers at the community pool. That was before she had gotten ill.

Their last summer together, they didn't make it out there once.

He stood for a few frozen moments peering through a small window in the door at the vast pool. It seemed to be a good crowd, and though he was without his glasses and couldn't make out faces, he was relatively sure most of them were seniors. No seventeen-year-old walked that slowly.

As soon as his feet crossed the threshold, he was quickly bombarded with a herd of the over-seventy gang who seemed to come out of nowhere. They had apparently been awaiting his arrival.

"Walter." Walter turned to the right and found himself staring into a curly mop of gray hair. It was Adolfo. The two had known each other for the better part of forty years. He had never married, but Walter and Gina would often double date with him and his lovely for the month—literally. Adolfo couldn't seem to hold interest in anyone longer than the thirty-day expiration date that Gina labeled his little trysts. "My friend, we are so glad you agreed to come and join the group."

"Believe me, I'd rather not. But the O'Callahan kid can be extremely annoying. I more or less surrendered. Agreement didn't have much play in the decision."

"Well, good to see you're still your fun-loving self.

Come on, we'll go and get in the water."

Stepping cautiously and being mindful of the wet surface, Walter followed Adolfo. He recognized most of the beaming faces around him.

"You're gonna have a great time. You'll feel a lot better after a few days in the water."

Rolling his eyes in irritation at the voice echoing from behind him, Walter tried to ignore the man submerged in the water and grasping a paddle board.

The senior crowd nicknamed him "Fish," but Walter thought Dory better suited him. Norman always reminded him of that character in the Disney movie *Finding Nemo*. Sweet guy, but about as sharp as a marble.

Ryan plopped in the water with his *friend,* Grace. No one officially stated Grace was more than that, but Walter suspected she was his girlfriend by the way they were glued to each other. Well, that and the fact he saw them kiss on the porch of Ryan's house a few weeks ago. But who was he to meddle? That was their business. He could see Ryan's mouth moving, but he didn't hear any of the words. He was too busy searching the pool for Lillian. She was the reason he was there, and of all of the faces surrounding him, hers was not one of them.

Tony Trash swam up beside him and punched Walter in the upper arm. Walter waded through the waist-deep water to turn and see who could have been so bold. When his eyes met the weathered and disproportionate face, his body stiffened. Tony Trash had earned his name because he couldn't stop his ongoing rude and unwanted comments about the women. It was something that always baffled Walter and Gina. To look at him, he hadn't been blessed with good looks at all. In fact, his features were unusually large and awkward for the size of his head. Something that always made Walter snicker under his breath. He never liked the man and only tolerated him because Gina, being the kind soul she was, asked him to. He stiffened his brow and glared at Tony, who continued to yap at him anyway.

"Walter, you need to tighten the circle and listen to what Ryan's saying. You're not going to know what to do."

"Mind your own business. I'll do what I want when I want. Now go bother someone else."

"I was just trying to help you, but if you're feeling out of place here in the pool, then why don't you go hang out with the old hens on the steps. That is, if there's room for you. They seem to be quite the plump crowd today," Tony quipped.

Walter was about to raise his fist to meet Tony's obnoxious mouth and rearrange his face, hopefully for the better, when someone in the distance caught his eye. He squinted, trying to see the face clearer, but it didn't help. Wading through the water, he pushed, growing closer to his destination and the singular figure. The closer he came, the better his depleted eye site could focus. There she sat, stark white luminous shoulder-length hair. Her tiny frame included shapely legs that kicked back and forth in the water. She was gazing up at the glass ceiling as if she saw something so wondrous she dared not look away. Her skin still had a glow for its ninety-two years, and her cheeks were surprisingly rosy. *Hmm...* Walter thought, *Lillian doesn't look upset or depressed.* He was nearly beside her when her gaze lowered to meet his eyes. She laughed, almost in a whisper, and tossed her hair back. *Nope, definitely didn't seem depressed.*

"Walter. You old devil."

"Lillian, my dear. How are you today?"

"Happy to see you. Where have you been? I haven't seen you around in such a long time. Not since ... Never mind. How are you?" Lillian scooted closer.

Walter was now perplexed. Ryan had been clear about her condition, and here she sat, looking and sounding perfectly fine. "I'm okay. The old bones are cracking more and more, but you know, all in all, I'm good. It's the nitwits around me that really ruin my day." He shot a wrinkled face toward Tony.

"Oh, don't let that fool bother you. He'll never change, and it's not worth your frustration."

"Did you hear about Elsa?"

"No. What happened? Is she alright?" Her smile faded.

"I don't know. They took her away by ambulance yesterday. Frank said she had stopped breathing.

I'd been waiting all night to hear something, but Vivienne was going to the hospital this morning. So hopefully, we'll know something soon."

"Poor Frank. She is his entire world. It's rough when it's only the two of you, and there are no children." Walter lowered his head and turned away. He knew Robert and Vivienne would be faced with the exact same issue someday. "Oh, Walter, I am so sorry. I didn't mean anything—."

"No. It's okay. I know you didn't, and you're right.

If this goes badly, Frank will be a lost soul."

"Well, now that I've managed to make myself a complete nuisance to you, I feel I should ask, how are Vivienne and Robert fairing?"

"They're getting through each day, as the saying goes, one at a time. Honestly, though, I don't know how either of them gets out of bed. And you're not a nuisance. Never have been and never could be. You were the first one to come to the house after Gina passed and the last one to leave. You're a good woman. Lillian Grainger, and Gina loved you."

"I loved her too. And how she put up with your crotchety old disposition for all those years, I'll never know. They've probably made her a saint up there. You know that, right?"

Walter laughed. It felt good to forget, even if only for a moment. "Well, my darling, you want to join me in this ridiculous waste of time taught by two people barely out of diapers?"

"You go on ahead. I'm going to sit this one out today," Lillian gestured towards the exit doors with her eyes.

Walter eyed her grip on the railing; she held it so tight her hands were losing color. Each step she took was a hurdle. He kept her in his sight as he treaded back to the group. She sat down halfway to the exit and rested before continuing to leave.

Class was every bit as miserable as he thought it would be. But he needed to stay, so he might as well get through it. When it was over, he waded through the water to the steps. Ryan was waiting for him, with Grace practically joined at his hip.

"I don't know what you've done here, boy, but you better start explaining. And more details this time."

"What do you mean? I saw you speaking to Lillian. Did she say something?" Ryan glanced over at the other seniors in the pool.

"It's not so much what she said. It's what she didn't say, or, rather, do. When I first sat with her, she seemed fine. Better than fine. She was very lively, happy. But toward the end of our conversation, it was like someone flipped a switch. She could barely walk, and not more than a few minutes earlier, she was kicking her legs in the water. So … tell me what's going on. And this time, you better tell me everything."

"Okay. You go change. Me and Grace have to clean up here, and I'll come by after dinner tonight and explain everything to you."

"No. Why can't you tell me now?"

"Because I made a promise."

Walter studied Ryan's face. He could see pain in Ryan's stiff jaw and tense stare. The kid meant business. Walter figured if it was that important to him, then it must be something he should abide by. He shook his head in agreement, and they parted ways.

Walter decided to wait out front for Vivienne. The brisk air felt good on his skin; it was invigorating. His thoughts traveled back to the days when he and Gina would take their boys to the beach. They never had a lot of money, but they had the best times.

Gina packed lunches, and on the days they had a few coins extra, they'd stop for ice cream on the pier. Robert, Frank, and Richard could play for hours. In fact, Walter often had to hall them over his shoulder to get them to leave.

My mind is still young, thought Walter, but the body just wanted to go its own way. He had so much energy back then. So many years have passed so quickly. He would have liked to share more days at the beach with Chase … if he could have one moment back. Just one.

A tear trickled from the corner of his eye, stinging his cheek. The bitterness of the cold became apparent, and the feeling of life faded into the reality of the day. Walter turned and saw Vivienne's car pulling into the parking lot.

He quickly wiped his face with the handkerchief neatly tucked in his coat pocket and put on his best scowl. It was the best way he knew how to keep any more pain from crushing his family.

Walter walked up to the car and slid in. Vivienne had the heater on its highest setting, and the car felt more like a furnace than a haven.

"My goodness, woman. Are you trying to kill us by suffocation?"

"Well, hello to you too." Vivienne frowned and rolled her eyes. "Do you need me to lower it some?"

"I thought that was implied by my last statement. Is the cold freezing your brain? You need to take something like that Jinco Blaboba."

"You mean Ginkgo Biloba? I'm fine, Dad. The brain hasn't shut down yet. Although I have to say you do help keep it sharp," Vivienne smirked and lowered the heat, "How was class?"

"I'll never get that hour back," Walter's tone was gruff.

"Oh great! Glad to hear you had fun." Vivienne couldn't resist the sarcasm.

Walter let it go. His job was done … He made her grin.

Chapter Six

Walter had little interest in dinner, but that wouldn't stop Vivienne from pushing the calories on him. The question burned in his mind about Lillian. *Why was Ryan being so secretive?*

This was all very perplexing and damn annoying. Walter wasn't in the mood for games. Not today, or any day for that matter. He quickly cleared his plate and went to sit in the living room to wait for Ryan.

About forty-five minutes later, there was a knock at the door. Walter got up as quickly as he could, but Robert beat him to the punch. Ryan entered the room before Walter could complete the journey. He mumbled discontent under his breath. After all, he may be slower, but he wasn't feeble. He waved his arm at the sofa signifying to Ryan he should sit. Ryan gave Walter a nod and took his place. After a moment or two, Ryan leaned forward, clasped his hands, and rested them on his knees. Walter couldn't help thinking that he looked like he was about to hammer out a play in a football game.

"First of all, thanks for coming today, Walter. I know it meant a lot to Lillian because she told me. I needed to wait to speak with you because I made a promise to her. I needed her permission to let you know what is really going on." Ryan squirmed.

"Just spit it out, kid." Walter was losing patience.

"Lillian has bone cancer."

Walter gasped from the pain in his chest.

"Walter, are you okay?" Ryan stood up. "Should I call Robert?"

"No. Sit down. I'm fine." He rubbed his heart in a circular motion. "Tell me everything."

"She found out a few weeks ago. I guess she had been weak and feeling more body pain than usual. Her daughter took her in, and after some tests, she found out it was cancer." Ryan looked down.

"What are they doing for her? Is she getting chemo?" Walter anxiously rubbed his hands.

"Uh. No. Lillian has chosen to not have any treatment."

"What? Why not? I need to talk to that woman."

"Walter ... no. It won't do any good. Her entire family has tried, but it isn't what she wants. She told me that at her age, she'd rather have the time to enjoy her family and friends without the consequences of chemotherapy or radiation. She said she's had a long, great life, and now it's time to move on to another adventure."

"That does sound like Lillian. Headstrong and ready for anything," Walter cleared his throat.

"So, are you going to keep coming to class? I think she really needs all her friends around her right now."

Walter glanced up at the photos of first Chase and the other grandkids, then to the wedding picture of him and Gina. God, they were so young. A road of countless possibilities, a lifetime still yet to live. But his friend's road had come to an intersection, and she chose the path less traveled. He wouldn't let her take it on her own.

"I'll be there. But from now on, you have to be completely honest with me. I won't say anything to Lillian. It's up to her whether or not she chooses to share this with me, but you, that's an entirely different story. You hear any news about her condition worsening, miracle cure, whatever it is, I want to hear about it. Got it?" Walter glared at Ryan.

"I do, and I will. Promise." Ryan stood up. "I'll see you tomorrow, Walter. "

After Ryan left, Walter stood by the window and watched as he walked home. *He's a good kid,* he thought. *Still, an idiot like most of them, but this one has a heart.*

The phone rang, and he could hear Robert talking to someone. He made a reference to the game, and Walter concluded it was Richard, his middle son. Gina had given birth to two boys about three years apart. Frank, who was the eldest, and then Richard. Robert was referred to back then as a change of life baby and a complete surprise. Gina was forty when she found out she was pregnant. Frank had just turned eighteen, and Richard was fifteen. By the time Robert was five years old, both brothers had moved out of the house. Surprisingly though, they remained fairly close to their baby brother.

When it came to sports, that was the bond that kept them linked through the years. Especially Richard and Robert. They were the baseball nuts. Walter waited until he was sure the conversation had ended before going into the kitchen. Robert was fixing a cup of coffee. A late-night habit that sometimes kept him up and tired the next day.

"Was that Richard I heard you on the phone with?" Walter poured a small glass of orange juice. Something he was only allowed in moderation because of his diabetes.

"Yeah. We're going to James's game on Saturday. It's been a long time since you've seen your grandson play. You should come." Robert took a swallow of coffee and winced.

"Careful. You know that's hot," Walter chuckled.

"Thanks for the heads up. But really you should come with us, Dad. We can go to lunch after the game. It'll be fun."

James is Richard's youngest son and Walter's clone. His looks mirrored his grandfather so much that they often teased him about being a mini Papa.

"I don't think so. It's too cold." Walter placed his empty glass in the dishwasher.

"What do you mean it's too cold? You sit outside on the porch every day in twenty degrees." Robert shook his head.

"That's different. I can come in if I need to. You go and tell me all about it when you get home."

Robert walked out of the room without another word being spoken. Walter knew he had disappointed his son, and yet he didn't feel the need to rectify it. He wasn't going—end of story.

The rest of the evening was uneventful. Vivienne had stopped by the hospital earlier in the day as she had planned. Elsa was in a coma and not responding. Frank was by her bedside holding her hand, and Vincent had brought him a burger and fries from the cafeteria. Vivienne urged Vincent to go home and rest. She won out after relentless coaxing.

After an hour of nothingness on the fantasy box, Walter opted to go to bed. He was worried about Lillian and unsure what he could do but decided he would go to the pool every day during the week. He was sure Vivienne would go along with it. She'd probably think he was enjoying himself, and she'd love the idea he was socializing.

Hey, whatever it took to get him there, he'd let her believe what she wanted. He was going strictly for his friend; if Lillian was there, he could at least keep her company.

After changing into his pajamas and doing his usual *business* before bed, he laid his glasses on the nightstand and shifted his body until it was neatly covered under the feathery comforter. Saying his usual nightly prayers, he added one more to the list, Lillian. Hesitating, he made his final request ... please, Lord, not that dream tonight.

Walter opened his eyes to a buttery, bright room. He had slept through the entire night. No dream and no bathroom trips. A double oddity for him. He didn't care. He felt rested and a little exhilarated. Sitting up, he looked around the room and squinted.

Stretching for his glasses, he thought, *After all these years, why do I still do that?* He chuckled softly.

After the usual morning routine, he settled down on the living room couch, fully dressed and ready to go. Vivienne's mouth hung open when she came down the stairs and saw him waiting.

"You're ready to go?"

"Yup. Have been for about thirty minutes." Walter checked his watch.

"Did you eat breakfast?"

"Yup."

"How about your insulin? Did you take your injection?"

"Yup."

"Do you have your towel and pool shoes?"

"What am I, a child? Yes, yes, and yes. Can we go now?" Walter stood up and reached for his cane propped up against the couch.

"Sure. Just let me grab a cup of coffee to go." Vivienne hastily made her way to the kitchen.

Walter stood tapping his foot. He was anxious to get to the pool. Hoping Lillian was there, he had brought some of the old pictures they had collected over the years. He had known most of the neighborhood since they were in their twenties when he and Gina first bought their house. It was so quaint and only a few blocks away from where he lived now.

A small white cape style with black shutters. He and Gina thought it was important that if they were going to raise kids, they needed a yard to play in. The house only had two bedrooms, so when Robert came along, they took some money out of their equity and added a third bedroom. He missed that house.

"Okay, I'm ready," Vivienne slipped on her heavy winter coat hanging from a hook by the front door, "I think it's really chilly today. Or at least that's what the weather report stated last night. I'll be glad when spring gets here."

"Whatever. Can we go now?"

Vivienne turned away. Walter went to apologize, but as usual, he couldn't. So, he opted for silence.

When they arrived, he noticed Lillian's old nineteen-eighty Cadillac parked in one of the back spaces. His heart palpitated, and his palms grew moist. When Vivienne pulled up to the front, Walter swiftly opened the door.

"Come on, you have to wait until I stop the car." Vivienne placed the car in park and proceeded to get out.

"Where are you going?" Walter was irritated.

"I thought I'd come in with you. The sidewalk looks a little slippery." She grabbed her purse from the floor on the passenger side.

"I don't need you. I can walk twenty feet on my own. Now, thank you for the ride, but please go home. I'll call when I'm ready to be picked up." Walter slammed the door and cautiously walked toward the entrance without looking back.

Once inside, he went to the front desk and checked in. The Twinkie Twins, a name he came up with for the two teens, were at their post.

"Hello. How can we help you today? Are you checking in for a class?" The young boy smiled.

"You just saw me yesterday, right?" Walter leaned on the counter.

"Yes, sir. I remember you."

"I was here for a class yesterday. I think it's a pretty good bet I'm here for one today too."

"I ... uh ... yes. If you could just sign in, please." The boy's face glowed red.

Walter pushed through the door to the locker room. He liked to find a locker toward the back where there was more privacy. Stepping slowly to avoid a fall, he eyed each row until he found the one that suited him. There were wooden benches for the members to sit on or place their belongings. Walter did neither of them. He opened his locker and placed his bag inside. Then he removed his jacket and set it in the locker next to his bag. Piece after piece went into the locker, each one pristinely folded. He then unzipped his bag and removed his pool shoes and towel. Holding onto the row of lockers, he put on his shoes one at a time before closing the door. He slipped the key into the pocket of his swim trunks and buttoned it closed before wrapping his lower half with the towel.

"What's the matter, Walter? You afraid to touch the bench?"

Walter hadn't noticed the gentleman sitting on the bench in the row across from him—Harry Henry. A horrible name his parents chose but an all-around nice guy. Lucky for him.

"Oh, Harry, I didn't see you there. You're damn right; I'm afraid to even put my things on that germ-ridden hunk of wood. Guys put their wetsuits on there; God knows what sort of disease they might have."

"I see your point. I guess I'll just have to live on the edge," Harry smiled.

"It's your ass. Do with it what you want. You heading in or leaving?"

"Heading in. Evelyn is already in the pool. She left early this morning to catch that water aerobics class the kids are teaching. Me, I've had enough lessons in my life. I'd rather relax in the morning and take my time. You know what I mean, Walter?"

"I sure do. Vivienne and Robert feel the need to school me constantly. Sometimes I think they forget who the parent is. Two pains in the asses, that's what they are." Walter grabbed his cane and ambled over to Harry. "How is Evelyn feeling? It's good she's here; things must be better."

"Thanks for asking. Yes. She's doing much better. I thought I was going to lose her there for a while, but she's a tough bird. She's so damn independent. If she had just waited for me to walk with her to the park, that driver had no right getting behind the wheel," Harry looked down as he shook his head.

"Well, glad to hear she's getting better. That's what really matters. I'll see you in the pool."

"Okay, Walter. I'll be there in a jiff."

Before entering, Walter assessed the crowd through the small square window in the door. The pool was clear, but the crowd was enormous. Every one of the lanes for the deeper end was filled with teens. Walter figured they were from the swim team. They usually came here two to three times a day to practice. He had hoped he had missed them. Apparently not. He opened the door and struggled to hold it open. He swore it weighed a hundred pounds.

When he was at the pool's edge, he rubbed his nose, trying to ease the sting. *Too much chlorine,* he murmured to himself. He glanced toward the senior class to see if Lillian was possibly there. She wasn't. In the distance, sitting on one of the chairs watching the kids compete, was a fragile figure. She wore a one-piece black suit and large brim hat—Lillian. The only woman Walter knew who could wear a hat like that to an indoor pool and not look ridiculous. He set his towel down on a nearby chair and slowly walked over to talk with her. When he was close enough, she greeted him with an animated wave of both arms and a huge smile.

"Walter. Walter. Come here and sit with me." She pulled the adjoining chair closer to hers.

Walter's step quickened to keep up the pace of the exhilaration coursing through his once-tired body. He couldn't stop smiling. Not even if he tried.

"Lillian. You look lovely today." He took a seat next to her.

"Well, back for day two. I must say, Walter, you've surprised me. I thought for sure yesterday would be your first and last day." Lillian reached for a cover-up in her bag.

"Are you chilly? I can get my towel. It's just over there." Walter pointed.

"No. I'm fine. Caught a breeze, but this is working perfectly."

"So why did you think I wouldn't be back?" Walter adjusted in his seat to face Lillian.

"I know this isn't your thing. But I'm happy you decided to return. You're much more interesting to talk to than Tony Trash and a heck of a lot more fun than Norman."

They both laughed.

"Are you going in the pool, Walter?" Lillian looked around the facility.

"That depends."

"On?"

"You."

Lillian smiled. "Do you think if you get into the warm water, you may feel better?"

"Perhaps. Let's go see."

Walter stood up and put his arm out for Lillian to grasp. The two sauntered to the pool and gently eased down the stairs and into the three feet of almost tropical water.

"Oh, this does feel good. Walter, you were right. It's much warmer in here."

"I think it's hotter than yesterday " Walter ducked down, letting the water cover his shoulders.

Lillian swam arms straight in front, pushing the water away like parting the Red Sea. Walter watched her. She really was very tiny, much thinner than he had ever remembered. What she needed was some of his Gina's home cooking.

If she were alive, she would have definitely had Lillian over for dinner, and if she didn't feel well enough to come over, she'd have brought it to her.

"She's not looking so good. Like a shriveled piece of fruit, you know when the skin ripples and hangs there. Don't you think so?"

Walter pivoted around. He recognized that nasal, high-pitched voice. Tony Trash. The Grim Reaper of etiquette sounded like helium crossed with a bad head cold.

He glared at Tony and then turned away without saying a word. If he only knew how sick Lillian really was. Today he was in no mood to feed into his abusive and useless opinions.

"Hey, Walter. Did you hear me? I think Lillian is on her last trip around the block."

That was it. Walter couldn't hold his tongue. He tried to ignore him, but Tony was making it impossible. He had trashed-talked every female within a fifty-foot radius for as long as Walter could remember. He especially hated it when Tony would make remarks in front of Gina. Although she never needed his rescuing, his spicy Italian had a mind of her own, and she didn't hesitate to share it with Tony on more than one occasion.

"Shut up, Tony, and mind your own business. It never ceases to amaze me how you always have something bad to say about every woman you see.

I wonder, is it because they take one look at that ugly mug of yours and turn the other way? I'm serious. Have you taken a long look in the mirror lately? Because I need to tell you, you didn't start out winning any beauty contests, and it certainly hasn't gotten better through the years," Walter continued.

"You've always had the kind of face that could break a mirror, and now it's just a sagging mess. Now how does that feel, buddy?"

Tony's jaw dropped. First time since he's known him, Tony Trash was at a loss for words. Walter smirked as the man shuffled to the exit and disappeared.

"What the heck did you say to that man?" Walter turned to see Lillian floating behind him.

"Nothing. We just came to an agreement," Walter cleared his throat.

"And did this agreement involve him traipsing out of here like he just lost his puppy?"

"Something like that."

"Good." Lillian treaded over to Walter. "He's always such a miserable soul. I've tried making decent conversation with him for years. But I gave up. He is the most negative person I have ever met."

"My Gina used to give him hell. I enjoyed watching it." Walter grinned.

"She was a lovely woman. I miss her terribly. And yes. She could be very feisty. A trait that I adored."

Walter decided to move on with the conversation to something else. Spending too much time discussing Gina reminded him of the loss he could never replace.

"I had an idea if you're up for it?" Walter raised his brows.

"Well, that depends."

"On?"

"On what your idea is."

"My daughter-in-law, Vivienne, is a great cook. You know that, though, because you've had many of her dishes during the holidays."

"Yes, Viv's a marvelous cook." Lillian swam to the nearby steps and sat down.

"I was thinking you should come over for dinner. Maybe a night next week?" Walter sat on the step above her.

"And does Vivienne know about this invitation?"

"Well, no, but I'll talk with her tonight. But I know she would love to have you."

"You know Walter, it does sound lovely. You let me know, and I'll be there."

"Excellent. We can confirm tomorrow. I should be here about nine a.m."

"Tomorrow? You're coming back again? Well, aren't you full of surprises lately, Mr. Reilly."

"You'll be here, right?" Walter shivered. "I guess I will. Are you getting cold?"

"Yes. It's chilly when you're not in the water."

"Well, that's my cue because I'm cold too. How about we dry off and go back to the chairs." Lillian stood up and wrapped her fingers around the handrail.

"Sounds good to me."

Walter slowly took the stairs and reached for his cane lying beside the pool. He walked with Lillian to their seats and wrapped himself in his towel before sitting down.

Lillian had brought a soft blue terry cloth robe and wrapped it close with the attached belt. They spent the next two hours reminiscing and going through the old photos that Walter had brought with him.

He was having such a good time he didn't realize how late it had gotten. Lillian was growing tired, and they agreed to talk more when they met up tomorrow.

Walter called Vivienne before changing, knowing it would take her a few minutes to get there. When he finished dressing, he walked out to the front door and waited inside the lobby for her to arrive. He smiled to himself when he thought about the past few hours. It had been the best day in a very long time.

Chapter Seven

Lillian Abigail Johnson was born June twenty-fourth, nineteen hundred and twenty-eight. Her father was an attorney for a large canning company, and she came into the world with the pleasures of privilege. A debutante ball at sixteen, the best education, and a job with her father's firm, all before the tender age of twenty-three. She was animated, opinionated, and brilliant. All the attributes a woman needed in the business world and was condemned for.

At twenty-five, she married the love of her life, Sam Grainger. A man neither her mother nor father approved. Sam was a blue-collar worker in the steel industry, and given her background, they thought he was beneath her. Lillian chose to ignore their prejudices and live her life on her own terms. They, in turn, dissolved her trust and split it between her two younger siblings. Lillian didn't care. She had Sam. They were going to make a life together with children, dreams, hopes, and many friends. One of the things that Lillian loved so much about Sam was his willingness to talk to anyone. He could travel three states away and still meet someone he knew. It was so different than the censored life she had grown up with.

Financially life wasn't easy in the beginning. Two daughters, a small house, and any dog or cat they could rescue from the cold spread their income thin. Lillian learned to cook large meals on pennies and use the leftovers to create additional meals.

When both girls were in school full-time, she decided it was time to get back into the working world and help out.

Not knowing what she wanted to do, Lillian decided to try her hand at the one thing she had enjoyed immensely over the years—photography. It was a hobby she had developed to document the life of her family. She started soon after her first daughter, Emily, had been born, and by the time Lois came along, Lillian had grown quite good at it. She was able to capture and share things that Sam would have missed being at work. The first few steps, a funny expression, playing in the park, or an excessively messy piece of chocolate cake. It gave them permanent memories and she loved that.

In the beginning, she started with her close friends. They'd schedule a session, and she wouldn't charge. It gave her the experience she needed working with others rather than only family. It wasn't long before her pictures caught on, and she was receiving requests from word-of-mouth referrals. Lillian tried to add not only the memory of what she captured in a sitting, but life. Instead of only the traditional stoic poses, she had her subjects engage in silly activities like pretending to be playing charades. Their happiness was forever snapped in a Lillian Grainger photo. She was a hit.

Through the years, her notoriety grew. As did their finances. They traded the little house for a four-bedroom, three-bath colonial with a yard almost as large as the park she grew up playing in. Life was good.

Then one evening on their thirtieth wedding anniversary on, the way to an intimate dinner for two, it all changed in seconds. It had been raining, and Sam was driving slowly. He had suggested they cancel and go out another night, but Lillian had been looking forward to it all day. She had given herself a manicure, set her hair in curlers for added wave, and put on a new black dress she was saving just for that night.

A little rain was not going to stop Her. But on the way to the restaurant, that little rain turned into a torrential pour. Sam could barely see through the angry sheets of water that hit the windshield, rendering his wipers useless.

The car came to a rest at the two-way stop sign on Plainfield Ave. The illumination of the sign through the watery haze meant they were only a block away from their destination. The misplaced, rectangular advertisement was above the front door of the restaurant and designed to resemble the marquee at a movie theater—Opening Night—based on the owner's philosophy every dining experience should mirror the perfection of premiere night. The name did little justice to the upscale cuisine served once you passed through the large mahogany doors.

Sam looked to his right and then his left before proceeding through the intersection. What Sam nor Lillian didn't see was the car making a left-hand turn from the opposite corner. The wall of water had been so dense, the other driver never saw their vehicle. . . until it was too late. In seconds her life was shattered.

Warm liquid trickled down over her right eye as she reached up to touch her throbbing temple. Her fingers traced the outer edges of what felt to be a large gash. She wiped her hand on the front of her coat. Twisting to free her body from its painful position of being smashed against the passenger door, something was pinning her.

"It's okay, lady. You're gonna be fine. We're getting you out."

Lillian looked up, and through the flashing lights, water drops danced and settled into a blurry reflection on the shattered glass of the windshield.

The tall, burly man wore a yellow slicker that bore the initials FDNY. Lillian immediately realized what had happened. They were in an accident, and the fire department was there to help them. Them—*where was Sam?*

Her mind went into a frenzy as she struggled to turn, but the weight of whatever was pinning her would not let her budge.

"Listen to me. What's your name?" The man was crouching down to the window.

"Lillian," her voice trembled.

"Lillian, my name is Ralph. I'm going to remove the door handle with a blow from this sledgehammer. Don't worry, you'll be okay, but I need you to try and keep your face off the glass. Can you do that?"

Lillian winced and nodded in agreement.

By the third blow, the door was opened, and she gasped as two large arms surrounded her and slid her out onto the ground. The rain peppered her exposed legs, and the stinging cold surged straight to her hips. Lillian placed her hands on the asphalt and pushed to get her body to cooperate.

"Sam. Sam! Where's my husband? Is he alright?

Did you get him out, too? Please! Someone help him!"

Ralph tried to calm her, but Lillian wouldn't stop. Pushing him away, she tried lifting up again, but this time, the ache turned into a shooting pain through the right leg. Inspecting her thigh, it was fine until she got to her shin. A piece of bone had torn its way through her skin and was jutting out almost two inches above the break. Lillian convulsed and turned to the side, vomiting violently in the street.

Lillian grew closer to the stars, her body weightless as she was placed on a gurney and into a waiting ambulance.

Two days later, she woke up in a hospital bed, her right leg in a cast, six stitches in her head, and the news that the weight pinning her in the car had been that of her deceased husband.

That day Lillian made a pact with God. If he didn't bother her anymore, she wouldn't ask him for anything ever again. That was their last conversation.

The next few days were the most enjoyment Walter had had in a very long time. He spent several hours a day at the pool talking with Lillian and the added benefit of getting in a little exercise. Lillian made sure they both had water time.

She said that at their age, they needed to stay as active as possible. If they didn't, their parts just might freeze up. Walter thought that was funny. In fact, she made him laugh quite often. Another new for him lately.

Friday came and went, leaving Walter with his *dreaded* Saturday—the one day every few months Robert and Vivienne forced him to attend a family dinner with Vivienne's brother Jim and his family. He had been lucky. The last few times they let it slide, and he stayed home. But now that he was getting out and spending time with Lillian, they told him there were no excuses. He could spend time with family as well. Walter surmised that because Jim wasn't his blood, he really wasn't family. But he'd never say that to Vivienne.

The car ride to Jim's was about thirty minutes away. Walter didn't mind it all that much. He sat in the back seat and was alone with his thoughts. It gave him the calm he needed before the storm.

Unfortunately, today was one of those days Vivienne decided she would try to make awkward conversation to relieve the awkward silence. Lucky him.

"Dad, are you warm enough back there because we can turn the heater up?" Vivienne adjusted the center vent.

"I'm fine." Walter rolled his eyes.

Walter faced out the window, hoping she would leave him alone. It didn't work.

"Samantha baked your favorite cake, German chocolate."

Samantha was Jim's wife and a supreme baker.

"Thank you, but I know what my favorite cake is, and it's lemon," Walter snapped.

"Stop it. Vivienne was trying to tell you that Samantha had done something nice for you. How about you just say thank you."

Vivienne continued as if nothing negative had been said.

"I forgot to tell you, I spoke with Frank this morning. There's no change with Elsa. He sounds exhausted. I told him I would go by on Monday and bring him some lunch. He's been sleeping there. The poor man is lost without her."

"I'd like to go with you when you do," Walter softened his tone.

"Sure... We can stop by the deli and get some sandwiches, and all have lunch together. It'll give Frank a break. Plus, I'm sure he would be thrilled to see you."

"Well, I wouldn't say thrilled, but I think it's a good idea I go and see them both." Walter was afraid it would be the last time he saw Elsa.

When they pulled up to Jim and Samantha's, the kids were playing basketball in the driveway with the new Little Tykes hoop that Robert and Vivienne had gotten them for Christmas.

Jim was overseeing the kids' match and walked over to greet his sister at the car. After they all unloaded, he whistled for the kids to go inside. The lawn still had a thin layer of snow, but the driveway and street were clear. Walter walked slowly and steadily with his cane. He was worried about patches of ice. The last thing he needed was to be next to Elsa in a bed.

As soon as they walked in, the aroma brought him back to winter Sundays graced with Gina's cooking. It was the best day of the week as far as he was concerned. No chores, no outings. Just time with his kids and beautiful wife.

Samantha was a sweet soul. Walter didn't voice it, but he had thought it from the first time he met her. In fact, he often wondered how Jim was so lucky to have landed such a catch. He and Samantha had met at work. They were both attorneys at the same firm before Samantha had decided to try her hand at opening up her own practice. It was extremely successful, and a few years after they married, she sold it for a considerable profit.

Walter wondered if she had ever regretted trading the lifestyle of a professional for a *Suzie homemaker*. She always appeared happy, so he assumed she was. Like Vivienne and Robert, Jim and Samantha had their kids a little later on in life. Samantha was thirty-three before she had Derek and thirty-six when Sadie was born.

Walter thought it was harder having kids when you were older. Thinking back to all the times he spent roughhousing with the first two boys, it was a breeze in his twenties and thirties. But when Robert came along, it was a different story. By the time he was old enough to roll around and wrestle,

Walter was nearly fifty. He didn't have the same stamina and felt maybe Robert missed out on some things that his brother didn't.

Dinner had a few more minutes left until it was ready, and Jim took everyone's drink order. Walter opted for a bourbon with ice, no water. Vivienne frowned, but he didn't care. He hardly drank anymore and would need it to get through this dinner.

On their mother's orders, the two kids had gone in and washed their hands.

They both came barreling into the living room and landed on Walter's lap. Derek had just turned seven a month ago, and Sadie was almost five. Walter adored both of them, but for a while, it had been too painful to see them, and he preferred a little separation. He set them down on the couch next to Robert and scooted over.

"There. Now the two of you have some room to stretch." Walter sat back.

"Uncle Water, look at my new book." Sadie grinned.

"That's very nice. Can you read it?" Walter wiped his palms down the sides of his trousers.

"No. But you can read it to me."

The little girl handed the book to Walter.

His heart thumped vigorously and sweat formed above his lip and the back of his neck. His hands shook, and the book slid out of his grasp and onto the floor.

"Hey. You dropped my book, Uncle Walter." Sadie picked it up and wiped it off.

Walter glanced at Vivienne, who was watching the child try to hand the book back to Walter.

"Sadie. Come here. Let me see your new book. Uncle Walter is tired; we should let him rest."

Walter breathed a sigh of relief as the little girl skipped over to Vivienne. A moment later, Jim gave the dinner call.

Walter kept to himself. He barely heard the conversations pinging back and forth between the other four adults. The kids were focused on trying to appease their mother by eating enough dinner to gain them a crack at the German chocolate cake she had baked.

Hovering under the table, Charlie, the Scottish terrier mix, was patiently waiting, hoping someone would either be careless and drop a morsel, or be kindhearted and share. Walter tore bits of his corned beef off and slipped some to the patient white puff.

After they had all finished and cleared the table, Samantha brought out coffee and cake. She handed Walter the first piece, and he thanked her. Upon close inspection, Walter was reminded of the cakes in the window of the bakery downtown. He took his fork and swooped in for a healthy chunk. Placing it in his mouth, he let the cake melt, blending all the flavors into one heavenly bite. It was delicious. Although he was not about to let Samantha know how good he really thought her baking was, he did nod and murmur it was fine. Robert glared, but Walter just looked away.

He didn't want to be there, and they made him come along. As far as he was concerned, he didn't have to be all giggles and grins. He reached to the side table where Samantha had set his coffee.

It was in a dainty little flowered white cup with saucer. Walter hated his coffee in anything other than a mug. That's what coffee was meant to be served in.

Not a little china *going to lunch with the ladies* sort of cup. No. Those cups were for tea and pretentious fancy-pants. His fingers struggled to navigate through the delicate handle. After one sip, he gave up. He figured he'd wait and have his coffee at home—where there were mugs. The time droned on, and Walter found himself staring at his watch. It was seven-thirty, and he had outlived his allowance for patience and grace.

"Robert. I'm very tired, and I'd like to go home now." Walter stood up and steadied himself with his cane.

"Dad. We're having a nice time. Samantha cooked a delicious meal and baked especially for you. The least you could do is have a little patience and let us enjoy ourselves for a little while longer," Robert continued his conversation with Jim.

Walter huffed and sat back down. He would wait thirty more minutes—no more.

With eight chimes ringing from the dining room clock, Walter abruptly got up and walked to the front door. He grabbed his coat from the rack and bundled up. When he was done, he walked out the front door with a wave, a quick thanks, and goodbyes. He crunched through the snow that had fallen and covered the driveway during dinner. Coming to a halt at the car, he sighed loudly and waited. It wasn't long before Robert and Vivienne came out, yelling their thanks and offering hugs and kisses.

Robert didn't say a word. He unlocked the door and got in. Sitting in the driver's seat, he waited until Walter had belted before taking off. Walter knew he was angry but felt no need for apologies.

If they wanted to stay longer, they shouldn't have brought him in the first place. Correction, they should not have *forced* him.

When they got home, Robert went upstairs and didn't emerge for the rest of the evening. Vivienne was her usual diplomatic self and tried to get Walter to go and speak to him. Walter would not. After about three rounds of banter, she finally gave up and went to bed.

Walter sat in a dark living room. He didn't want any light; he desperately needed the shadows. His mind floated, blending with the abyss and then becoming calm. He wondered if this was what death felt like. To be in a vast space of nothingness, always quiet. He would welcome that. Maybe he and his Gina could be together, and ... Walter's body shook as the salt trickled over his lips and stung. He pulled his handkerchief out and wiped his face. It was time for bed.

Chapter Eight

The pool was deserted the next morning. Lillian wasn't there, and Walter decided to sit and just watch. He hoped she was okay; maybe she was just tired. Norman and Adolfo were engaging in conversation by the side of the pool and shouted for him to join them.

"Not today, boys. I'm going to relax in my chair and enjoy some peace."

Unfortunately, that wouldn't last. Walter felt a hand on his shoulder and turned to find Harry taking the seat next to him. Walter sighed.

"How you doing, old man?" Harry grinned.

"Fine." Walter twisted his body to face the other way.

"Evelyn's not feeling well today. But like a trooper, there she is doing her exercises."

Walter turned back to face him. He liked both Harry and Evelyn and hated hearing she was under the weather.

"I'm sorry to hear that. Should she be in the pool?"

"Honestly. I don't think so, but there's no telling her that. That's one of the reasons why I come. I'm afraid to let her be here alone when she's like this. I'd rather be watching a movie in my nice warm living room." Harry smirked.

"I hear you. The place is kind of empty today. I was thinking of calling Vivienne in a few minutes to come and get me."

"No need to do that. Evelyn's nearly done. She'll be wrapping it up in a few minutes. We'll drop you home."

"Thanks, Harry. I appreciate it."

"No problem. You're on the way home anyways." Harry got up. "I'll go see if I can't hurry her along. She might leave quicker for you," Harry laughed.

Walter nodded.

In less than a half hour, Walter found himself standing in his living room with Vivienne shocked to see him there.

"How did you get home? Why are you home? Are you feeling alright?"

Walter rolled his eyes. "Calm down. I'm fine. You don't have to break my eardrums with that shriek. The pool was dead, so Harry and Evelyn gave me a ride home."

"Why didn't you call me? I would have come and picked you up." Vivienne frowned.

"Harry offered, and I accepted. No reason to call you." Walter took off his coat.

"Do you want something to eat? I made some cinnamon rolls."

"Sure. Is there coffee?" Walter sat in his usual chair. "Yup. I'll set you up at your chair."

When Vivienne said she'd set you up, that meant she was taking a TV table out from the hall closet. Walter never understood why she didn't just leave them out. But she was the cook and the housekeeper, so he let it go.

Vivienne brought the table first and then disappeared into the kitchen. Walter could hear her clanging around and turned the volume of the television up. His hearing was getting worse. The more background noise there was, the harder it was for him to distinguish what was being said. He knew there were words, but his trouble was understanding the words.

Knowing this would send Vivienne right into a full-blown doctor frenzy, he decided upping the volume was the best way to handle it.

The aroma of cinnamon trailed along the room as Vivienne came in with a plate of two buns and a mug of coffee. She placed them on the tray and sat down on the couch.

Walter rolled his eyes. This meant she wanted to have a conversation. Why couldn't she just let him enjoy his food in peace?

"I wanted to talk to you about going to the hospital today."

Walter didn't say anything. He waited for the punchline.

"I spoke with Frank when you were at the pool. Elsa is ... Dad, she's not going to recover. They are taking her off of life support later today. And Robert and I think it might be best if you don't go and see her. You know, remember her the way she was before this happened."

Walter spit out his piece of cinnamon roll, nearly missing the plate.

"You and Robert don't think it's good? Who are the two of you to tell me what is and isn't good for me? Let me remind you who the parent here is. The two of you don't tell me what to do. Elsa is my friend. Frank is my friend, and I know how hard this will be for him. I'm going whether you take me or if I have to call a cab. Either way, I will be at the hospital before they remove those damn wires." Walter's hands shook with anger.

The audacity, he thought. He fiercely pushed away the tray sending coffee spilling all over and onto the carpet. He didn't care. He needed to get some air and get away from her before he said something far worse. He grabbed his cane and coat and walked out the front door. Instead of stopping and sitting on the bench, this time, he kept going.

It was several blocks before he began shivering. His breath left his mouth in a puff of steam. He had to cover his cheeks with his hands to ease the stinging. Gazing up at the street sign, he found himself at Clarence and Pansy. Five blocks from home.

Walter knew he had better get back before the cold got the best of him. He had been so angry. It was beyond thinking that a man his age had to be treated like a five-year-old child by his own kids. If Gina had been there, she would have given them an ear full. Unfortunately, he lacked her finesse for relaying emotions. Lately, all he felt was bitterness. He wanted to tell them how sick he felt inside. How every day was a victory if he got out of bed. How a conversation with most, even the simplest or mundane, was an effort that took all his energy. In fact, the only one he had enjoyed talking to in a long time was Lillian. He felt like his old self with her.

Taking a step off the curb and into the street, his cane hit a small patch of ice and slipped. The pale blue sky and splash of clouds were his new landscape. Lifting his head, he felt a sharp pain in the back of his neck. Feeling around for blood, there was nothing. With his right hand, he glided over the road, searching for his cane. His fingers touched the tip. He struggled to reach until it was in his grasp. Slowly pushing his body up with his left hand, he rolled onto his side and took a few moments to gather strength.

He was halfway up when a car stopped abruptly in front of him.

"Oh my God! Are you okay? Can you move?" Vivienne nearly fell out of the car trying to get to him.

Walter didn't want to tell her how happy he was to see her. In fact, he held back the tears threatening to give away his secret. But this time, he did let her help him. She reached under his arms and pulled him up while he pushed with his legs. Once steady, she kept a firm grip on his arm until he was in the car.

Nothing was said on the way home. In fact, nothing was said for the next few hours. Walter sat in his chair watching episodes of Gunsmoke on one of the obscure cable channels, and Vivienne stayed in the kitchen.

He had no idea what she was doing in there, but whatever it was, he felt she needed the break as much as he did.

At four o'clock, Vivienne came in and announced it was time to go to the hospital. Walter bundled up for the twenty-minute ride to Bethlehem Memorial.

Elsa was on the fourth floor in ICU. When they reached her room, Frank was standing at her bedside holding her hand. His eyes were swollen and red. Walter ambled over and stood beside him. He kissed his hand and then gently touched Elsa's forehead. Then he placed his hand on Frank's shoulder and stood with him in silence until the doctors came.

Walter whispered to Vivienne, "I think we should leave."

She nodded.

"Frank, it's getting crowded in here and they're probably gonna throw us out so we're gonna go. If you need anything, please call."

Frank gave them both a tight hug and kissed Vivienne on the cheek. "Thank you both, for everything."

As they turned to leave, Walter noticed Frank's older brother Anthony walk in and inch his way to the corner of the room.

When they were back in the car and on the way home, Walter couldn't hold his voice any longer.

"She looked very peaceful."

"Yes. She did. I'm glad Anthony showed up." Vivienne softly smiled.

"Me too. I didn't want to leave Frank alone. I know they wouldn't let us stay because we aren't family." Walter frowned.

"You alright?"

Vivienne quickly glanced at him and then turned her attention back to the road.

"I'm okay."

Walter turned away but couldn't control it this time. The tears flowed down his cheeks, and he covered his face with his hands.

Vivienne reached out and clasped his hand. Walter held on tight until the wave of emotions settled. He cleared his throat and wiped his face with a paper towel from Vivienne's stash in the center console. When they got home he went straight up to bed.

Walter looked up at the nozzle pointed at his chest. He closed his eyes and waited for the explosion. He felt a jolt, and then strangely, he felt nothing.

Sitting up, he frantically searched the room. He was alone and chilled. It was moist under the palms of his hands, and his sheets were soaked from sweat. His pajama shirt stuck to his back, and he wrestled to get the buttons open and get it off. Throwing it on the floor, he swung his legs over and into his slippers.

His cane was hooked to his bedside table, but when he reached for it, his shaking hand couldn't grip tight, and it slipped through his fingers.

Walter sat on the edge of the bed staring at the cane on the floor. Fists down, he used his arms to lift his body slowly. When he was in a prone position, he painfully straightened his back. Hobbling over to his dresser, he took out a dry shirt and slipped it on. He couldn't maneuver the bed sheets to change them, so he decided to sit in his recliner by the window and go back to sleep. Vivienne would change them in the morning.

He tugged the comforter off the bed and sat down. When he was reclined, he pulled it over his body and glanced out of the window. He struggled to push back the lump in his throat whenever he thought about his dream. He would have been perfectly okay if he had not woken up in the hospital that day. He had been resolved to his fate. What he was not right with was the fact that he did wake up. This was a cruel punishment. As he closed his eyes, he took one last gaze at the heavens and spoke a silent prayer for death.

Walter woke to a repeated loud rap at the door. "Dad. Are you awake? Can I come in?" Robert's voice sounded stressed.

"Come in."

Robert looked at Walter in the chair and then at the wet stain on the sheet.

"The dream again? "Robert's voice softened.

Walter nodded.

"Listen, I wanted to tell you that Vivienne's not feeling well today. Some kind of stomach thing. I can take you to the pool if you get ready. But you'll need to find a ride home."

"Not to worry. I've decided to stay home today. I can help Vivienne."

Robert's eyes were wide, and his mouth gaping. "Uh. Yeah. That would be great. Well ... okay then. If anything happens, just call me at work. I'll try to get home early."

"I got this. Don't worry." Walter stood up.

Robert noticed the cane on the floor. He picked it up and handed it to his dad.

"Thank you. Now go. We'll be fine." Walter shooed him.

After Robert left, Walter went to Vivienne's room and listened. It was quiet, so he let her be and went downstairs to fix breakfast. The doorbell rang shortly after eleven a.m., but by the time Walter got up and opened it, the only thing greeting him was a small package.

Walter scanned the label. It was addressed to Vivienne from John Adams Elementary school. Walter's breathing became shallow, and he grabbed the wall to hold himself up. Clutching his chest, he saw darkness.

"Oh my God!"

Walter heard Robert in the distance. He was frantic. "Please, please. Don't do this. No, no, no."

Walter pushed on his eyelids, forcing them to flutter and then open.

"What happened?" Walter labored to get up.

"Let me help you." Robert let his father use his arms to hold onto as they both worked to get Walter up and on the couch.

"I came home for lunch to check on you two and found you passed out on the floor. I thought you were dead."

"No such luck."

"Dad!" Robert huffed.

"I'm fine. Just a dizzy spell. It happened after I read the label on the package for Vivienne."

Robert looked around and saw the brown square on the floor in the entryway. He picked it up and read the label. Walter watched all the color drain from his son's face.

"I'll give this to Vivienne when she's feeling better. Not today."

Walter nodded.

"I think you need to see the doctor. You fell yesterday, and maybe you were hurt more than we thought." Robert was still examining the package.

"No doctor. And don't bring it up again."

Walter turned on the television and raised the volume. He hoped Robert would take the cue. He did. First, he went upstairs to check on Vivienne and then straight to the kitchen. When he finally came out, it was because he was leaving to go back to work. A quick goodbye, and he was out the door.

Walter sat back and rested for the remainder of the afternoon, glancing only once at the box on the bookshelf.

The wait was worse than the inevitable outcome he was bracing for. Time quietly moved on with each passing day, slipping through his fingers like sand.

Walter didn't go to the pool, and neither did most of his friends. They were all mentally preparing to say goodbye to Elsa. The wake was held at St. Hedwig's Catholic Church, but Walter chose not to attend. Frank decided on an open casket for the three-day viewing, a Church tradition. Walter couldn't bring himself to see such a lovely lady motionless in a wooden box. On the day of the funeral, Vivienne had laid out his black suit with a light gray shirt and charcoal tie. He thought a second about scoffing that he could take out his own clothes, but he didn't. It would take too much effort, and he just didn't have any to spare.

Walter rode to the church with Vincent Dalo. He'd rather be with his friends right now instead of the watchful eyes of Vivienne and Robert. Vincent was dressed in a brown suit. A fashion choice Walter found to be inappropriate for a funeral. As far as he was concerned, black was the only choice to show respect.

The church was crowded. A testament to the kind of person Elsa was. Everybody loved her. The pulpit was surrounded by white lilies and yellow roses.

Elsa loved yellow roses, and the lilies were a funeral tradition in the Catholic Church. Walter and Vincent took a seat two rows behind the family. Harry and Evelyn had saved a space for them in their pew.

The priest came in from the vestibule in a procession with two altar boys and a young deacon new to St. Hedwig's. Walter couldn't remember his name, but he thought the young man had a face with character. His features resembled more of a boxer than a holy man. His nose was crooked and leaned to the left like it had taken several hits from a powerful fist. He also had what they refer to in the boxing world as *cauliflower ears*, a distortion that occurred when the ears were repeatedly subjected to right jabs.

When the brigade reached the altar, the two boys took a seat on the left side and the deacon on the right. The priest stood at the pulpit and proceeded to say Mass. Walter had hoped to skip this ritual, but he wasn't so lucky.

When Mass was finished, the priest prompted those who wanted to speak a few words about Elsa to come up. Tony Trash was the first to go up, and Walter cringed. But to his surprise, Tony kept it short and only said kind words. One by one, his friends followed and said their piece about the friend they didn't want to say goodbye to. Walter didn't go up. He knew how he felt; he had no need to share. Finally, Frank stood up. He wobbled, and his brother held his arm and walked him to the pulpit. He stayed by his side while Frank spoke of the love of his life. He shook as the tears flowed uncontrollably. Walter struggled to keep his own composure. Short breaths and the squeezing of his thumbs were the only things keeping him from a complete breakdown.

Once Frank was done, Anthony escorted him back to his pew. The priest spoke the closing words and then gave them directions to the grave site. Walter leaned to Vincent to ask him if they were going, but Vincent shook his *no* before Walter had a chance to say a word.

The two waited until everyone had existed before getting up, genuflecting to the altar, and leaving.

When they were in the car, Vincent was the first to speak.

"I'm sorry if you wanted to go to the gravesite; I just couldn't," Vincent cleared his throat.

"No. I was going to say the same thing. I don't want my last memory of Elsa to be seeing her lowered into the ground."

"Yeah. That's exactly what I was thinking. Frank's in a real bad way. Did you see Anthony hold him up at the pulpit?"

"I saw him help him up and stand next to him when Frank spoke. Is that what you mean?" Walter turned to gaze out the window.

"No. When Anthony was standing beside him, he had his arm around his back."

"Oh. I didn't see that. But he is barely making it. He looked as if he'd aged ten years in a week."

"Yeah. I know. Poor guy. He's going to have a rough go of it. I won't be surprised if his is the next funeral..."

"Stop! Don't say it. We just buried one friend. Don't put another one in the ground so soon," Walter's face grew red.

"You're right. Sorry." Vincent frowned.

"You hungry?"

"Yeah. I could eat a bite. Pizza or sandwiches?"

"Pizza. Vivienne rarely gets it. She's worried about my cholesterol. I swear if I watched my eating like she wanted me to, you might as well put me in a box. I'll call her and let her know not to worry about dinner. We are eating out." Walter smirked.

The best in the neighborhood was at John's. It didn't sound very Italian, but John Tattori had been making pizza for over forty years.

He had mastered the crust like no one else, and his sauce was the perfect blend of tomatoes, basil, garlic, and whatever else he secretly used to get it to taste so good. The restaurant was small, and Walter liked it that way.

When the guys walked in, John was in his usual place behind the counter.

The brick ovens were behind him, and he had two rounds of pizza dough stretched out and waiting for toppings.

"Boys! How the hell are you?" John smiled.

"Not so good, my friend," Walter and Vincent took a seat at a table near the counter. "We just came from Elsa Taylor's funeral."

"Oh. I know that was today. I'm so sorry. I had my delivery girl bring over five large pies to Frank's. I thought it might help."

"Good man. I'm sure he will greatly appreciate it." Walter put his glasses on.

"What are you boys having tonight? The pepperoni special?" John put the pizza in the oven.

Walter turned to Vincent. "I think I want a pepperoni, but also some calzone."

He was helpless against the lure of those small, folded delights with mozzarella, sausage, ricotta, sauce, and spices. It was the best part of pizza but bundled into a neat package.

"You know what, that sounds good," Vincent chuckled.

"John, we'll take the special and add a meat calzone to the order."

"Whoa. You two must be hungry. A special and a meat calzone coming up."

Walter loved watching John twirl the dough. It reminded him of the last time he took Chase out to lunch. They had spent the day in the city at Radio City Music Hall for the Christmas show.

Afterward, he took Chase to a tiny pizza parlor off the main street. Walter had found it by accident one day when he was in the city meeting an old high school friend who had come in for a few days.

Chase loved it. He was a little pizza monster—had been ever since he was old enough to eat food that wasn't in a baby jar. It was one of their best days next to Disneyland, of course.

Walter allowed himself to relive the emotions of the day, reigniting the exhilaration he had once felt. But as he allowed himself to give in, he was quickly reminded of the other day. The one that would change everything. His throat felt thick, and it was hard to swallow. He wiped his forehead with a napkin and grabbed a drink of ice water that John had set on the table. Gazing around the restaurant, the sound muffled, and his body tensed. He was having another attack. He was shaking vigorously ... *was he convulsing*? His mind raced.

"Walter. Hey buddy. You okay?" Vincent's voice cracked.

"Yeah. Yeah." Walter realized it was his friend shaking him back to reality.

"Whew. You scared me there for a minute. Where'd the hell did you go. I was practically shouting your name. It was like you couldn't hear me." Vincent waited.

"I was remembering that day I took Chasey to the city."

"Oh. I'm so sorry. I know that was a great day for you two." Vincent fidgeted with his napkin.

"It's okay. You're right. It was a good day." Walter took another sip of water. "I'm starving."

"Here you go, boys. I can't wait to see if you can finish all of this," John laughed.

"I'd better. It'll be the last time I get it for a while.

Vivienne runs a tight kitchen." Walter grinned.

Dinner was thankfully uneventful. They finished their entire meal, much to the surprise of John. Afterward, Vincent dropped Walter off at home.

Getting ready for bed that night, Walter thought about Elsa. She had been the cutest little thing with a kind, gentle nature. Not unlike the heart of his Gina but hers came with a vivacious Italian beauty. He hoped they both shared a special place in heaven.

As he got under the covers and closed his eyes, he saw Elsa's face. Not the way she looked in the hospital, but in her youth, when they all still had a lifetime to live. As the sleep swept through his body, his mind traveled to his vault of memories. BBQs in the yard, holiday drinks at the Taylor's, and Sunday gravy at home. Time was winding down, and soon the clock would stop. Walter smiled.

Chapter Nine

Walter waved as Vivienne pulled away. Finally—she didn't try to get out and walk him in. After his usual routine of paying for the day and changing into his swim trunks, he pushed through the doors to the pool with determination. Lillian would be there. He knew this because he called her that morning to be sure. He would spend as much time with her as she would allow.

Elsa's death had taken his breath away. He hadn't had much conversation with her over the past few months, and he hated himself for that. He spent time with Lillian to make sure that didn't happen again.

Lillian was sitting on the middle step in the shallow end of the pool. She was gliding her legs through the water and gazing out across the floor and up to the ceiling windows that surrounded three of the four walls leading to the pool area. Walter hobbled over to her, set his cane down on the cement, and stepped in while grabbing the railing to steady his descent. Lillian peered over and smiled. She didn't utter a word. Walter took the cue and simply sat with her.

He enjoyed this. Too many times, people felt the need to converse even when they had nothing of substance to say. He would prefer quiet contemplation in a person's company than struggling for words that didn't need to be found. Alas, not everyone shared Walter's view.

"Hey Walter, what are ya doing?"

Walter cringed. It was the annoyingly abrasive voice of Tony Trash.

"Walter. Hey, did you hear me? What are you two doing over there?" Tony was standing at the top of the steps.

"What does it look like, Tony? We're waiting for a bus." Walter's tone hinted at sarcasm.

Lillian giggled, and Walter grinned. "What do you want?"

"Nothing. I'm coming in. Move over." Tony grabbed the railing and stepped in.

"There isn't room enough on this step for all of us. Why don't you go wading in the pool?" Walter scooted away a few inches from Lillian, taking up the rest of the step.

"Nonsense. I can sit on the one below you." Tony coughed.

He had smoked at least a pack a day for the last fifty years. His cough sometimes caused him to spew out saliva, and if you weren't quick and he forgot to cover his mouth, you were a splash victim.

"Cover your damn mouth Tony," Walter scolded. "Oh, sorry. Did I get you?" Tony sat down and wheezed.

"No. That's what we're trying to avoid." Walter knitted his brows.

"How the hell are you, Lillian?" Tony splashed the water.

"I'm quite fine. How are you?" The corners of Lillian's mouth creased.

Gracious as usual, Walter thought. *This buffoon doesn't deserve it.*

"Not so good today. My arthritis is pretty bad in both knees. The doc said the water should help, but it's got a hold of me today. All those years jumping out of planes, I guess."

"Tony, I had no idea. You were a paratrooper?" Lillian scooted herself around to face him.

"Sure was. Both Korea and Vietnam. One hundred-one airborne with a total of fifty-seven jumps. I loved the flying; it was the landings my body had issues with," Tony laughed.

"My brother Ellis served in Korea. He was a proud marine. Never spoke of his time in combat, but we knew he had seen things that changed him." Lillian looked away.

"Yeah, things were definitely not like here. How about you, Walter? Were you in the service?"

"Why would you ask such a stupid question?" Walter snapped.

Lillian frowned at him, and he shook his head. "Tony. Don't you remember? I saw combat in Korea. We were both at the community center when they had the veteran's luncheon honoring all the local guys."

Tony scrunched his face, and Walter could see he was struggling to remember. *Maybe Tony Trash wasn't as well as he appeared to be.* Walter took a deep breath and let it out slowly.

"Wait. I do remember. We had burgers and hot dogs with the best damned potato salad I ever had. You got up and gave a short speech, Walter. It was very good. Later, we all got plaques with our service dates on them and our branch of service." Tony grinned.

"That's right," Walter sighed.

"I forget things sometimes lately." Tony looked down into the water.

Lillian reached out and took his hand, "That's okay. We all do."

Walter started to think that Tony wasn't so bad. Sadly, as fate would have it, the next few words to pass by his lips were typical Tony Trash.

"Hey, Walter, look." Tony pointed to a large woman at the other end of the pool. "Doesn't Miriam Smith have all the makings of a beached whale in that black bathing suit?" Tony laughed.

Walter couldn't give credence to Tony's words. Instead, he asked Lillian if she'd like to go and sit by the windows on a lounge chair. She agreed so quickly that Walter figured she must be as repulsed by Tony Trash as he was.

Once settled in their new Tony Trash free-zone, Lillian was the first to break the silence.

"I know he gets to you, Walter."

"What do you mean?" Walter was curious.

"Tony. I know that he bothers you considerably. His mouth is foul. I'll give you that. But he is a lost man. There are reasons why he is so obnoxious in his thinking. His hurt runs deep."

Walter was shocked by her willingness to make excuses. "He is always so degrading to women. Sometimes men, but mostly women. How can you make excuses for him?"

"My dear man, you should know better than most what it feels like to be ripped up inside. There are days I have seen you with Vivienne and Robert that weren't the best representation of your character."

"I know I can be short and sometimes rough, but I've never been degrading." Walter was bothered by her opinion of his shortcomings.

"I know that. I'm merely saying that everyone has a story and don't judge until you know the whole truth." Lillian reached out and squeezed Walter's arm.

"Then please ... tell me Tony's story."

"I can't." Lillian shook her head.

"Why not? You talk as if you know it." Walter frowned.

"I do."

"Then ... "Walter leaned forward.

"It's not my story to tell."

"Then how do you know?"

"Tony and I grew up together. I've known him since we were in the second grade."

"I didn't know that." Walter's eyes widened.

"Most folks don't. But I was around to see why Tony shaped into the person you see today." She glanced over at him.

"But I'm confused. You were surprised to find out he was in the service."

"We lost contact a couple of years after graduation. When he returned, I didn't ask where he had been, and he didn't tell me."

Walter sat back and mulled over everything Lillian had said. He was now conflicted. He desired to know the secrets of Anthony Camaratti's life that turned him into Tony Trash, but he was not about to ask him.

Anthony Joseph Camaratti came into the world on December twenty-ninth, nineteen hundred and twenty-seven. His mother and father were poor immigrants from Italy. When Anthony was three, his father was hired to lay steel for a skyscraper but died when he fell from the tenth story. His mother, a seamstress since she was twelve, lied about Anthony's age four months before his fifth birthday so he could start school early. She would tell him later it was the only way she knew how to be sure he was taken care of while she put in a full day's work.

Life wasn't easy without a father. His mother worked all the time, just managing to put food on the table. Anthony learned to keep himself occupied after school by earning a couple of dollars running errands and grocery shopping for old Mrs. Pellegrino. Her husband had passed away several years before, and they had no children of their own. Anthony thought she was helping him ease his mother's financial burden, and in turn, he did the things she could no longer do on her own. They both won. Besides, he liked her. She was kind to him.

As Anthony got older, he traded his formal name for Tony. He liked it better. He felt like a regular guy, and Tony was a regular name.

When Tony was sixteen his whole world changed. Bethany Poccelli transferred schools, and he was hooked at first sight. After several attempts to ask her out, she finally agreed after he made a fool out of himself in front of their entire science class. He stood in front of everyone and sang, *Did You Ever See a Dream Walking* by Bing Crosby. It was after that serenade they both agreed he should definitely not become a crooner.

Inseparable through high school, the plan was clear to Tony. He couldn't afford a diamond, so he purchased a simple opal from the jeweler's downtown.

On one knee, he professed his eternal love and undying commitment to her. They were married in September, three months after graduation.

Eight months later, Bethany found out she was pregnant with their first child. The couple was beyond happy. They had talked about having a big family, maybe five or six children, and this was their beginning. Their luck overflowed when they learned Tony got a promotion at work. He had gone from checker to assistant manager at B & B Groceries. Life was perfect.

Bethany was in her sixth month of pregnancy and determined to finish the nursery before the baby came. She had chosen neutral colors that would work for either a girl or a boy and would sprinkle blue or pink after their little angel arrived. Tony had finished painting the room the day before and had to go into work early that morning. Bethany had decided to take a walk downtown and look for nursery furniture. Tony had asked her to wait until he was home from work, but she didn't want to be a bother to him. She knew he'd be tired after a full day on his feet, and besides, she knew he would go along with whatever she selected.

The only baby store in town was about a fifteen-minute walk each way. Bethany convinced herself it would be good exercise. She had been feeling a bit like Humpty Dumpty lately. The weather was a modest seventy-five degrees, and the sun was shining. She put on her most comfortable flat shoes, a lightweight, short-sleeved cotton shift, and a pastel floral silk scarf wrapped around her head and tied in the back. Tony had teased her about her purse weighing more than she did. Although she would never admit it, he was right. But she couldn't part with any of the contents.

After all, you never knew when you would need a lipstick refresh, handkerchiefs, a bag of hair pins, a compact, camera, travel clock, stockings, pocketknife, and several other items that found their way into her possession. The most direct route was through two large intersections. They were usually at their busiest during the afternoon, but the alternative would take her ten minutes longer, and with her belly beginning to bulge, she'd rather a few more cars than minutes.

The walk felt good. The air was brimming with scents of lavender, lilac, and freshly cut lawns. The sun's rays found a nesting place on the apple of her cheeks, and Bethany gazed up to drench in the warmth. Her pace was slower than usual, but normally she weighed ten pounds lighter, so she didn't mind. When she reached the stop signs for the first intersection, she stood on the edge of the corner and looked to her right and then to her left. Surprisingly, there were no cars around. Looking both ways again, she stepped out into the road and quickened her pace until she was on the other side.

The remainder of the walk was peaceful. Coming to the second intersection, she felt slightly overheated and decided to stop at Monte's diner for a soda. The place was two doors down from the baby store, which made it perfect.

As she attempted to open the heavy glass door, a gentlemen leaving rushed forward and held it open for her.

She thanked him and took a seat on one of the many open stools. Monte was the owner and usually spent most of his time behind the counter.

"Good afternoon Mrs. Camaratti. What can I get you?" Monte wiped down the counter with a rag.

"Good morning Monte. Could I get a root beer and maybe some of your yummy vegetable soup?"

"Soup on a warm day like this?"

"Yes. Monte, didn't your mother tell you if you eat or drink something hot, it will make you feel cooler?" Bethany removed her scarf and set it in her purse.

"Nope. Can't say as I heard that one. Would you like crackers with that?"

"That would be very nice. Thank you."

Bethany glanced around the diner before taking a pen and paper out of her purse. She wanted to make a grocery list while she was in town. After the baby store, she would go to the grocery store and pick out what she needed. The store had a delivery boy, Bobby Ficeratto. He was a nice kid, and Bethany knew her order would be delivered within a few hours of purchase.

"Here you go, Mrs. Camaratti. Enjoy." Monte smiled wide.

"Thank you. I'm sure I will."

The soup was tasty, and she savored every drop while crunching on some saltine crackers. After the last swig of root beer, her belly was full. Now it was time to shop. As soon as she stepped outside, there was a loud bang from across the street. A car had pulled into a space in front of the hardware store and backfired. A puff of black smoke burst from the tailpipe. Bethany covered her nose as she quickly walked to the baby store.

Wilson's had been in business for over forty years. They had the best quality baby furniture and accessories for over a hundred miles. Bethany could barely contain her excitement walking through the door. Her eyes widened in wonder at the selection. She tried to focus on one item at a time, but she couldn't.

There were several cribs to choose from, and if you didn't see exactly what you wanted, Wilson's would craft one for you.

Bethany was greeted by an older saleswoman with white hair pinned up in a bun and a conservative black pantsuit.

"Can I help you?" The woman tilted her head and smiled.

"Yes. I need ... everything," Bethany laughed.

"Well. Then we better get started. Let me show you some cribs first. You can build the rest of the room around it."

"Oh, how sweet." Bethany clapped lightly.

After a couple of hours and several indecisions, Bethany found the crib, matching dresser, and changing table in a warm, light blonde oak. There was a creamy beige and white bedding set that went perfectly with the baby animal mobile she just had to have. And finally, six dozen diapers, pins, undershirts, and booties completed the list for their very special newborn-to-be. The store would have everything sent over in a week.

Feeling quite accomplished, Bethany set out to complete her day of shopping at B&B Groceries. Bobby was most helpful, and she finished the list in no time. He assured her he would have them at her front door in no more than two hours. Bethany thanked him and handed him twenty-five cents. She knew it was customary to tip afterward, but she liked to do a little before and then usually some after, too.

The streets were busier than when she left the house earlier, and she decided it was a better idea to take the longer, less congested route home.

There was only one main intersection that she needed to cross. It was a four-way stop but rarely were there ever four cars there at the same time.

She did exactly as before. She looked both ways, and then before stepping off the curb, she looked again. All clear. Quickly she hastened her pace and reached the other side before a car was in sight. Stopping to catch her breath, she wiped a bead of sweat from her forehead with a hanky from her purse. The pulsing ache in her legs weighed them down and stole her energy. Focusing on getting home and a bed to lie down on, she never noticed the cloud of black smoke and thundering boom before the out-of-control vehicle jumped the curb.

Tony was busy helping the box-boy bag groceries when Officer James Sherman from the sheriff's department barreled into the store and abruptly whisked him away to St. Anne's Catholic Hospital. He waited several hours while the surgeon worked on his love, Bethany. And then waited several hours more before he received the tragic news; mother and child were gone.

The funeral was held at Holy Trinity Catholic Church. Tony had his unborn daughter and her mother placed in the mahogany and cherry casket surrounded by lilies and white roses. The priest said a full mass and spoke of loss and reuniting someday. Tony didn't hear any of it. He didn't want to. *There was no reason for this. No grand plan that his beautiful wife and daughter were a part of in this life. There was only an inexperienced driver with a bad muffler who struck them down and killed them. Took them from him, and he would never, never see them again. They're not waiting for him in heaven with harps and white robes. They are motionless in a wood box that will be buried six feet under the ground and forgotten.* His thoughts plummeted to the depths of loneliness as he realized a life without his beloved wife and the daughter he would never know.

Over the next couple of years, Tony began to shut down and remove himself from anyone close to his life.

After the death of his mother, he enlisted in the army. He wanted to jump out of airplanes and test his fate, not the best goal for a paratrooper. After serving in two wars, he came home. An injury in Vietnam cut his tour short and only added to fuel the anger he had already felt.

His mother had left him their house, so he returned to the old neighborhood. Time had passed him by, and most of the people he once knew had moved away. He became a recluse, rarely ever leaving the house. Until the day a completely unexpected visitor knocked on the door. Lillian came over with some homemade beef stew. They shared a meal and then another, and another after that.

Over time with tenacity, Lillian introduced Tony to the world again. But he was never the same man. His anger consumed his soul and chipped away all the enthusiasm he had once felt for life. His loose lips and fowl commentary earned him the name Tony Trash. He once confided in Lillian that the words held no meaning for him. His connection with life had been severed long ago. His only regret was every excruciating moment he had with his memories.

Chapter Ten

The next day, Walter was more determined than ever to uncover the story behind Tony Trash. He couldn't or wouldn't ask Tony directly. Vincent had been in the surrounding neighborhood all his life. There was a good chance he either went to school with Tony or, at the very least, had heard about the accident and what happened afterward.

He quickly dressed and went downstairs for breakfast. Vivienne had left a note on the kitchen table telling him she had some early errands to run. His eggs and bacon were warming in the oven, and the bread and butter were on the counter for toast. His cup was sitting next to the coffee pot, and there was a plate, napkin, and utensil set on the table. Walter smiled to himself, S*he really was a keeper*. Even if he couldn't tell her.

Also, on the table beside his plate was the folded newspaper fresh off the press for the day. Every morning Robert picked the paper from the porch and brought it in for Walter to read. Both he and Vivienne preferred the digital version, but not Walter. He still enjoyed the familiar smell of the ink and the grainy texture of the fresh paper on his fingertips.

This morning was different, though. He had a mission, and his mind couldn't think of anything else. He ate quickly and barely glanced at the paper. After loading up his dish in the dishwasher, he put on his heavy coat and proceeded on his quest for information.

He shivered as he stepped onto the porch. The sky was a dark gray backdrop to the puffs of black and white. He took the steps slowly in case there had been ice from the night before.

Crunching on the smooth surface that covered the lawn, his footprints were like a map to the treasure he hoped to find.

The porch light was still on when he got to Vincent's front door. Walter hesitated before knocking in fear he might still be asleep. But after surmising that this late in the morning, it was more likely he just forgot to turn it off, Walter lifted the heavy brass knocker and let it fall. The substantial thud was followed by the click of the bolt unlocking shortly after. He knew his assumption had been correct.

"Walter. Is everything okay?" Vincent was still chewing.

"Yes. Fine. I was wondering if I could come and speak with you for a few minutes. Are you busy?"

"No. Just finishing breakfast and watching one of those morning shows. Damn boring if you ask me. Come on in." Vincent stepped aside to make room for Walter.

They walked into the living room, and Walter sat on the sofa next to Vincent's recliner.

"Would you like a cup of coffee?" Vincent took a sip.

Walter nodded. "Yeah. It's damn cold out. That sounds good."

When Vincent returned from the kitchen, he had a cup of black coffee and two biscotti on a plate. He set them down on a TV table to the left of Walter.

Walter wasn't hungry, but the biscotti looked appetizing. After a few sips of coffee, several passes at dunking and devouring the pastry, he was ready to get to business.

"You've lived here for a long time, right?"

"Most of my life. I was ten months old when my folks settled in the neighborhood. We used to live over on Navy Street." Vincent changed the channel.

"Did you know Tony Trash when he was a kid?"

"Sure. I went to school with him. Tony was two years older than me, but I'd pass him in the halls, and I knew who he was. Although most of us knew him as Anthony back then. Why are you asking?"

"I was wondering if you knew what happened to him after high school?" Walter took another pass at dunking the second biscotti.

"It was tragic. Tony was such a different guy back then. I know it's probably hard for you to believe, but he really was aces. Everybody liked him. He was super popular in school. He'd give you the shirt off his back if he knew you needed it. He started dating this really cute girl. What was her name ... uh, Bethany. Bethany Po ... damn, what was it ... Poccelli! Bethany Poccelli. She sure was a looker. Not in a Marilyn Monroe kind of way, but you know, a real cutie.

"They were married right after graduation. My parents were invited to the wedding, so I had to go. They were a great couple. It's a shame what happened to her."

"What?" Walter put down his cup and biscotti.

"Bethany was pregnant with their first child. Hell, I don't even think she was twenty yet. Anyway, she was hit and killed by a reckless driver walking home from downtown. The baby died too. A little girl. Practically the whole town attended the funeral. After that, Tony started to withdraw from everyone. When his mom passed a couple of years later, he joined the service. He went to Korea and then to Nam. That's where he got hurt. The crazy bastard jumped out of planes. When he got home, he never came out. The only way any of us knew he was still there was because of the grocery deliveries, and we'd occasionally see him mowing the lawn.

"Lillian was the one to get him back in action. But he wasn't the same Tony we all remembered. Not even close. I can't say that I blame him, but he really is just a shadow of who he was. I think sometimes he wishes he'd just die."

You know, maybe to be with Bethany and his daughter. Hell, I don't know," Vincent got up and took his coffee mug into the kitchen.

Walter went numb. He had no idea the tragedy that Tony had gone through. *How could I?* He still didn't like him, but now he understood.

"Walter, you want more coffee?" Vincent shouted from the kitchen.

"No. I better be on my way. But thank you for the coffee and biscotti."

Walter got up, and Vincent came out and walked him to the door.

"I'm curious; why did you want to know about Tony?"

"I don't know. Lillian had said he had a hard life, but you know Miss Lillian. She is forever tight-lipped when it comes to someone else's business."

"I guess we should all be thankful she is."

"What do you mean?" Walter cupped his hands and blew on them.

"Lillian has lived here and in the surrounding neighborhoods all her life. She probably knows more about each of us than we'd care to admit."

"On that, sir, you are correct. Take care, and thanks again." Walter waved as he stepped down onto the pavement.

When he heard the door shut, Walter paused. Gazing down the block, he eyed the houses of the neighbors he knew best and couldn't help wondering what secrets they were holding close.

It was almost noon when Vivienne came home. She was carrying several bags of groceries. Walter grabbed a few from her and brought them to the kitchen. He was tired from his morning espionage and told her he was going upstairs for a nap.

It didn't take long before his head hit the pillow, and sleep took him away, but his mind betrayed him. He ended up back in the middle of what he had been trying to escape for months—the bad place.

Walter looked at the clock on the wall above the dry-erase board. The chaos started just six minutes ago, but it felt as if hours had passed. He frantically scanned the room, now filled with crying and gasping children. Where was he? Turning his head the other way, he caught a glimpse of the red and blue striped shirt. He was nestled under a desk with two other children on either side. Walter thought about sliding over to him, but he knew he'd draw too much attention. The intruder was only about twenty feet away, and the last thing Walter wanted to do was to point him in his direction. The teacher, Mrs. Kendall, was shaking nearly uncontrollably. The intruder had her in his clutches and was yanking her head back by her hair. Walter started to move, but one of the kids in hysterics got up and ran for the door. He tried to get to her, but his knees wouldn't move fast enough to support his body. Bam! Bam!

A sudden jolt into reality shook off the horror his mind had been locked in. Sawing in a breath to slow the frenetic beat of his heart, Walter shivered and wiped away the tears streaming down his cheeks. He threw the moist pillow to the foot of his bed and stared at the ceiling, trying to bring himself back into focus. He was in his room and lying in his own bed, yet he still felt every sensation and emotion from that day. His body wouldn't stop trembling, his mind racing. The terror had taken hold once again.

Struggling to sit up, he threw the covers off and let his legs drop to the floor. It was ice cold and felt good on his clammy feet. Clearing his throat, he struggled to push back the thickness that had lodged itself on the back of his tongue. His cane was nearby, but he didn't reach for it. Instead, pushing off the bed with both fists clenched, he steadied himself with murmured curses and his own will. He was tired of feeling like he was dependent.

Tired of the nightmares and the lack of sleep. Tired of losing friends, and tired of his own life that had grown so depressing over the years. Hobbling to the window, he was surprised to see it was dark outside. He had slept longer than he thought. Great. As if his nights weren't plagued enough, he would be wide awake from getting too much rest during the day.

Going downstairs was inevitable. He needed a gulp of water to loosen the thickness in the back of his throat, and his stomach growled like a bear coming out of hibernation. He knew he'd come under scrutiny, though, and weighed the pros and cons. Surely Robert should be home by now. He glanced at the clock on his side table, six o'clock. Yup. No doubt, he was home. He'll probably start in about the nap and hitting his head the other day and how it was all a sign he needed to go to the doctor.

Walter sighed and contemplated going back and lying down on his bed, but his stomach let out a loud reminder that it needed to be fed.

Robert was watching the news from the recliner, and Vivienne must have been in the kitchen because Walter could hear the clanging of pots.

"Dad. I was just coming up to get you. Boy, that was some nap. You feeling okay? I told you we should probably make a doctor's appointment and have your head checked out."

Walter grumbled. He couldn't have written the dialogue in his head more precisely. Robert almost blurted out every word verbatim.

"I'm fine. Just need to rest. It's been a long couple of days." Walter sat on the couch.

"That it has. How was your sleep? Peaceful?" Robert got up from the recliner.

"It was fine."

"Here, sit down in your chair." Robert moved to the other end of the couch.

"No. Vivienne will probably call dinner soon. I'll stay here."

"Suit yourself. Hey, did you happen to read the paper this morning?" Robert reached for the folded paper that was on the coffee table.

"Never got around to it. Why? Don't tell me someone else I know passed away."

"No, nothing like that. There's an article in here about Lillian." Robert flipped the pages. "Oh, here it is,"

He folded the newspaper in half, leaving the article on top, and handed it to Walter.

"Huh. She's donating her summer home to the city for a shelter to be used for battered women and their children."

After reading the article, he sat back and laid his head against the cushion. He knew what this meant. Lillian was getting her affairs in order.

"Dinner, boys," Vivienne called. "Come on, you two.

It'll get cold."

She had prepared a roast, mashed potatoes, and green beans. Robert's favorite. "Robert, the gravy is in the kitchen in the pot. Will you pour some in the gravy boat and bring it in?"

"Sure."

Walter chuckled. Ever since he was a kid, Robert loved roast beef. Good thing Vivienne knew how to cook it to perfection.

"Vivienne, will you drop me off at the pool tomorrow?" Walter buttered a roll.

"Do you think it's a good idea? Maybe you should rest one more day before going back."

"I feel great. I want to get back in the water." Walter flashed a fake smile.

He looked up at Vivienne's knitted brows and knew that his bit about getting back in the water was probably what would sway her. If she believed that he was getting better physically, she wouldn't stop him.

"I'll agree to take you, but if you feel dizzy or anything else is bothering you, call me immediately. I'll come and get you right away." Vivienne locked eyes with Walter. " I'll be home all day tomorrow. There are some things I need to work on for the taxes. Which reminds me, I need to file yours for this year. I'll bring them with me to the accountant when I go in February. Please, get me all your papers."

"Taxes? I don't need to file those anymore. The guy told me that the last time we went, remember?"

"Yes, he did. But you cashed out part of that retirement fund, and that's added income you need to declare. It might not be enough to have to file, but I need to ask him, and I'd rather have all the papers than have to go back."

"Okay. Thanks. I'll get everything together over the weekend."

Walter took the plate of food from her hands. It was so full he wondered if his stomach growls had announced themselves to Vivienne.

"Great." Vivienne handed him the black pepper.

Walter put black pepper on everything, and roast beef was no exception. He even dusted a little over his mashed potatoes and green beans.

The dinner conversation was kept light and scarce, which pleased Walter immensely. He was in no mood for the droning sounds of the two of them whining about their day. He wanted peace, and for this dinner, at least, they gave it to him.

When dinner was over, Walter decided to sit on the porch for a few minutes. After arguing with Robert and Vivienne about the effects of the cold night air, he reached for his coat, scarf, and a wool blanket from the closet. After he was comfy in his chair, he gazed at the twinkling stars. They covered the darkness like a string of Christmas lights hanging from the archways in the house.

Vivienne loved Christmas, especially the little lights. She had Robert put them everywhere, both inside and out. Although the past few years, the house had been dark during the holidays, but before, they were the showcase of the neighborhood.

He heard a car pull up and turned to see Ryan's beat-up little Honda pulling up the driveway. Walter was hoping Ryan would just wave, but the way his luck was going lately, he figured the odds were against him. The boy got out of his car and retrieved a bag from the back seat. As Walter predicted, Ryan walked across the lawn and came up to the porch.

"Hi, Walter. It's really cold tonight." Ryan rubbed his hands together.

Walter nodded in agreement. Maybe if he didn't say much, the kid would catch the hint. No such luck.

"Have you spoken to Lillian today? I didn't see you at the pool this morning and I wondered if you had heard the news?"

The boy now had Walter's attention.

"Oh, Christ. Now what? Is she okay?" Walter's heart raced.

"Sort of. She had a reaction to the treatment they're giving her."

"Treatment?" Walter pulled the blanket up to his waist.

"I guess a relative convinced her to try chemo. She had decided no medical intervention. Personally, I think whoever this person is, they just wore her down. I don't think Lillian wants any of it."

"Is she in the hospital?" Walter shivered.

"No. They released her. She's home now. But I don't think she'll be at the pool for a few days. I thought you should know." Ryan got up.

"Thanks, kid. I'm glad you told me." Walter extended his hand.

Ryan grinned and clasped Walter's hand with a tight grip and firm shake.

"Goodnight."

Ryan quickly darted across the lawn and into his front door.

Walter once again lay back, gazing at the stars. *If Mohammed won't come to the mountain...* He would call Lillian in the morning and see if she needed anything from the store. A good excuse to drop by and check on her. And if she didn't, he was going anyway.

His breath was nearly crystallized by the time he decided to cut his porch time short. Neatly folding the blanket and tucking it under his arm, Walter was startled by Robert.

"Dad. Vivienne made some coffee. Would you like me to bring you a cup?"

"I was just coming in. Yes, I would like a cup. Are there any more of those little chocolate cookies that she picked up from the bakery yesterday?" Walter's eye twinkled.

"Sure," Robert chuckled, "I'll tell Viv to put some on a plate for you."

Robert held the door open, and Walter turned to squeeze by.

"Thanks. I'm going to wash up. I'll be in the kitchen shortly."

"No. Just go and sit in your recliner. Your show is going on in a few minutes. We'll set you up there."

"Show?" Walter strained to remember.

"*Criminal Minds*. It's a new one this week."

"Oh. I love that show," Walter exclaimed happily.

"We know you do. After you wash up, we'll meet you in the living room."

"Very good."

Walter quickly hung up his coat and placed the blanket on the shelf. *Criminal Minds* was his all-time favorite crime show. He had been watching it since it first aired in two thousand and five. He was a loyal viewer and a fact fountain when it came to the actors' background.

What a perfect way to spend his night. The channel was already set, the cookies and coffee were on his side table, and his comfy afghan was draped over the left arm of the chair. Walter settled in for an hour of pure intrigue.

The show, as usual, did not disappoint. Walter was swept up in its ability to both interest and horrify him at the same time. And, of course, at the end, as they did most of the time, the killer was caught. At ten o'clock, Walter switched on the news. After about ten minutes, he decided it was more gruesome than the show he had just watched and opted for laughter. There were old reruns of *The Benny Hill Show* on BBC, and he found himself quickly submerged into belly-aching laughter.

At eleven, he was tired enough to go to bed. The predictable ritual was to switch off the television, dim the overhead fan light, and quietly ascend the stairs to his room. Vivienne and Robert had gone to bed shortly after *Criminal Minds,* and he didn't want to disturb them.

Robert usually got up so early for work, and Vivienne never really slept anymore. What little she did get was plagued with nightmares. She never told him, but he often heard her yelling out in her sleep from his room.

He huffed when he remembered he'd never asked her if she would take him to Lillian's. He'd have to get her in the morning.

Walter changed into flannel pajamas and set his glasses on the night table. He squinted to look around his room. He preferred the blurry melding of colors over the shadows of the night. Lying down, it wasn't long before the veil of sleep blanketed his mind, and thoughts of Lillian replaced any others he was accustomed to having. For the first time in a long time, Walter was carried away to his dreams with a smile.

Chapter Eleven

The warmth on his right cheek was enough for Walter to open his eyes and greet a new day. Remembering he needed to ask Vivienne for a ride, he put on his robe, grabbed his cane, and ambled down the hallway to the master bedroom. The door was shut, and he hoped it meant she was still in there. Usually, when she's dressed, she leaves the bedroom door open.

Knock, knock. Walter tapped the door gently with his knuckles. He didn't want to startle her. Since it was bright out, he knew Robert had already left for work. The boy is out five days a week before the light of day and home after the sun has set. He had definitely inherited Walter's strong work ethic.

"Dad, are you knocking?" Vivienne's voice was groggy.

"Yes. May I come in?" Walter leaned into the door. "Sure."

Walter opened the door and walked about halfway into the room, keeping a distance from the bed.

"Is everything okay?" Vivienne sat up.

"Yes. I have a favor to ask you. Would you mind, if you have time, driving me to Lillian's today?" Walter felt uncomfortable and a little embarrassed she was still in bed.

"You're not going to the pool?" She yawned.

"No. Lillian's under the weather, and I thought I'd ask if she needed anything from the store, and then go over and keep her company. Oh, can we stop by the grocery store too?" Walter fidgeted with his fingers.

"I hope nothing serious?" Vivienne stretched.

"No. Just a little bug. I'll go get dressed and then make breakfast."

"Sounds good. I'll be down in a few minutes. And would you please take the butter out if you get to the kitchen before me?"

"Will do."

Walter couldn't leave the bedroom quick enough. He felt like he was intruding on his daughter-in-law's private space. After a warm shower, he dressed and put a dab of cologne on before going downstairs, *I have no idea why I used the cologne. I haven't had it on since Gina died,* he thought. *Silly old man.* He chuckled to himself.

Vivienne wasn't downstairs yet, so he took the butter out and set it on the counter like she'd asked. He was more of an eggs and bacon kind of guy when it came to breakfast. No need to take up any belly room with toast.

Walter fried two eggs and heated up some leftover bacon that Vivienne had put in the refrigerator the other day. Just as he was finished and about to sit down, Vivienne came whisking through the kitchen.

"Sorry, I seem to be really slow this morning. I'm walking around in a daze."

"You okay to drive me? I can maybe get a ride from Vincent." Walter took a fork full of egg.

"No. I'm fine. I can take you. I just need some coffee and a slice of toast. My stomach's a little queasy. It'll all go away, I'm sure of it. Must have been too much of that chocolate cake I shared with the girls at lunch yesterday."

Vivienne had two close friends. When she said, "the girls," she was referring to them. The three had attended St. Mary Gate of Heaven Catholic Grammar School and had been friends ever since. Walter was glad she had them to lean on.

They were with her through every minute of heartache, and he knew she would have never made it through half of it without them.

"How are your friends?" Walter finished the last bite of bacon.

"They're great. I miss not hanging out every week, but everyone's so busy. Loraine landed a new job at the hospital. She's in administration now and working her tail off. And Carla, she's working in admissions for Hofstra University."

"Sounds like they have their plate full."

"Yup." Vivienne buttered her toast. "Are we stopping at the market? I could use a few things too."

"Oh, I almost forgot. Let me call Lillian."

Walter stepped out of the kitchen into the laundry room and dialed. When Lillian answered, her voice was weak. The conversation was brief. No, she didn't need anything, but if he was stopping, some of the soup from the deli would be nice. The local market specialized in homemade soups. Although made in a deli, it was still delicious. Lillian requested the cream of chicken. It was a thick broth and loaded with chunks of white meat and vegetables with wide noodles. It was one of Walter's favorites too. He told Lillian he would leave shortly and stop at the market before he came over. When he hung up, he grabbed his chest. The twinge brought back the sadness he felt when they buried Elsa.

"Vivienne," Walter shouted from the laundry room. "We do need to make a stop at the market."

"Sure. I'm almost done. We'll leave in ten."

Walter went back up to his room and peeled a few twenties from his stash in the top drawer of his bureau. He hated plastic. What was the point? It was just another way for someone to steal from you. He tucked the bills into his wallet and then slipped the wallet into his back pocket. He went downstairs and bundled up before stepping out to wait on the porch.

He glanced over to Frank Taylor's house. He hadn't seen him since Elsa's funeral. It was time to stop by, maybe when he got home later. Vivienne abruptly opened the door, and it startled him. He swayed off balance for a second and caught the handrail surrounding the porch.

"You okay?" Vivienne reached for his arm.

"I'm fine. You ready to go?" Walter asked.

"Yes."

The two of them carefully walked to the car. It had rained during the night, and the driveway and sidewalks were covered in patches of ice. Walter held his cane up, not letting it hit the ground. The rubber tip was worn, and part of the wood was exposed. If he hit a patch of ice the right way, he'd go flying for sure.

"Dad. We need to get you a new cane. That worn-out thing is going to be the death of you." Vivienne opened the passenger car door.

"I don't want a new cane." Walter's face grew red.

"But you need one." She helped him into the seat.

"I said no. Gina bought me this cane, and Chasey used to…" Walter looked away.

Vivienne reached in and hugged him. Walter wiped his cheek after she pulled away. Not another word about the cane was spoken.

The store was crowded with all the early morning senior shoppers.

They always frustrated Walter because they slowed the checkout lines while fussing with coupons and freebies. He grumbled when he saw the lines, and Vivienne frowned.

"Don't. You know every penny counts for them. You were lucky; you had a pension. How many of them are like your friends on a fixed income?"

Walter rolled his eyes. He knew she was right, but he wasn't going to respond. The soup was fresh out of the pot and steaming. Walter beamed. Their timing was perfect.

The wait was as bad as he had anticipated. It was an inexperienced cashier, and she moved through each customer slowly. *This soup better be worth it.*

When they reached the car, Vivienne held the soup while Walter got in and buckled. She then handed the two large Styrofoam cups to him, and he placed them on his lap.

The heat penetrated through to his legs and started to burn his thighs. Vivienne grabbed a towel from the trunk, and as Walter lifted the cups, she laid the towel down over his knees.

"Better?" she smiled.

"Much. Thank you." Walter held them tightly.

The ride to Lillian's was plagued by pop music from the eighties and nineties, Vivienne's favorite. Walter winced. He could never understand how she could like this kind of music. He longed for the days of Bing Crosby and Dean Martin. He even enjoyed a little Elvis from time to time. They had lyrics, melody, and the right kind of stuff to make dancing a whole lot of fun. He and Gina enjoyed going out on Saturday nights when they were first dating. It was within their young budget, and everyone in the neighborhood was usually there too. A bunch of your friends and your girl... there was nothing better.

When they got to Lillian's house, Vivienne accompanied Walter to the door. She held the soup and he the box of assorted bakery cookies he thought they could both enjoy.

His friend's gray, gaunt face surprised him when she answered. When did it get this bad? he wondered. They embraced, and she took the box of cookies from him, freeing his hands to take the soup from Vivienne.

"Have a good time, you two." Vivienne waved as she walked to the car. "Call me when you're ready to come home or when Lillian kicks you out. Whichever comes first." She grinned.

The house was dark, and the television was the only source of illumination in the room. Lillian had been watching reruns of the old *Mary Tyler Moore Show*. She shuffled to the front window and opened the blinds. Picking up the remote, she turned off the television.

"So, dear friend, to what do I owe for the pleasure of this visit? Don't tell me another one of our friends has kicked the bucket. I'm running out of black dresses. Oh, that was awful. Sorry, Walter. Please tell me that isn't why you are here."

"No. Not at all. I hadn't seen you at the pool in a few days and thought you might be feeling a bit under the weather. There's nothing like a bowl of fresh soup and some bakery-fresh cookies to cheer a person up."

"How sweet of you. I really am sorry about the dying joke. It was in poor taste. I've been feeling a bit sad lately. There have been so many friends that we've lost the past few years. Honestly, I wake in the morning and ask the almighty, *why me*? How is it I'm still around and kicking when all those good people have gone? I tell you, Walter, it's a conundrum."

"My guess, Lillian, is you're not done here. Maybe the plan is for you to stick around a little longer while you finish up."

"Enough of this. Let's go into the kitchen and put this delicious soup into bowls. I have some nice crackers I picked up the last time I ordered my groceries. They really are very tasty."

Walter followed her to the kitchen with the soup in hand. Lillian reached into a bottom cabinet and emerged with two large soup bowls.

The bright flowers and festive design reminded Walter of a favorite Mexican restaurant where he and Gina often dined. Gina had loved anything spicy, and the dishes at La Mercado's definitely taunted her thirst.

Lillian carefully pulled off the lids while Walter held the containers so they wouldn't spill. He poured each one into a bowl, and Lillian grabbed the crackers from the pantry. She set out two soup spoons, a glass of water for each, and small plates for the crackers.

Walter pulled out the chair like a gentleman, and Lillian grinned and shook her head.

"Tell me, old friend, tiring of the pool, or is there something else?" Walter sipped his soup.

"No. I don't think I'd ever tire of going to the pool. I'm just having an extra few aches and pains lately. I'm going to be ninety-two soon. I think I've earned the privilege of some TV days." Lillian pursed her lips.

Walter took that as a cue to let the subject go. He knew how headstrong Lillian could be, and if she didn't want to mention her illness to him, then he needed to stop prying. The last thing he wanted to do was to annoy or offend her.

"You are one strong bird, Lillian Grainger." Walter bit a cracker. "Mmm. These are good."

"I told you. What did you think I'd lie to you? Silly old man."

"Old man. I'll have you know I'm in my prime." Walter winked.

"You're in your prime, alright. You're priming to get a kick in the bum by me," she laughed.

The rest of lunch was spent conversing about the past and the adventures they had both had. Lillian was far more traveled than Walter.

He got to see Korea during his service, but she had seen the world.

By the time she had turned twelve, her parents had taken her to most of Europe and the whole of Africa. Walter had asked her which destination had been her favorite. Without a doubt, it was Africa. She said she begged to stay. Her dad had to practically drag her on the boat screaming and kicking the entire way. When she was first married, they weren't as financially lucrative as her parents, but they managed to take a trip each year. Sometimes it was in the States, but their adventures went far and wide around the globe. For their tenth anniversary, they took a boat to Australia, a destination that most of their friends said they'd never do. It was too far and too undeveloped. They couldn't have been more wrong. She told Walter it was the most fun and exciting time she had spent on a ship. Australia was breathtaking.

Walter soaked in all the details about places he knew he'd never get to. He was content to see them through Lillian's eyes. He had the best life with Gina and the kids and was happy to have his roots remain firmly planted in the neighborhood.

After lunch, he helped Lillian clean up the dishes. She put on a pot of coffee and set the cookies out on a bone-white china plate.

Walter carried the plate into the living room and set it on the rectangular table in front of the couch. Lillian followed a few minutes later with a tray that contained two coffee cups with saucers and a sterling coffee decanter.

"I must be special; you broke out the fancy stuff for me."

"Don't get too excited. I bring this out for everyone," Lillian smirked.

"I see how you are. Teasing me with fine dining ware and then knocking me down."

"Walter Reilly, you are a pain in the ass."

"Ah, those words bring music to my ears. Gina spoke them often."

"I always said she was a smart woman."

Walter enjoyed dunking the little cookies into his coffee and sucking the liquid out of them. Lillian told him it was barbaric. He didn't care. He couldn't remember the last time he had enjoyed someone's company so completely. Lillian and Walter had little in common when it came to background, but their lives mirrored each other in many other ways. They both were devoted to their spouses and had a good marriage. Family was everything to them, and their friendships were forged in heart and soul. For a few hours, he had forgotten all the sadness that had haunted him the past year and a half.

It was about two o'clock in the afternoon when Walter glanced at Lillian and knew it was time to call Vivienne. Lillian's head bobbed back onto the cushion, and her lower jaw opened. Walter pulled his phone from his front pocket and went into the kitchen so he wouldn't startle Lillian. When he was finished, he gathered the dishes, cups, and saucers and placed them on the tray with the silver decanter.

He brought them into the kitchen. After he washed them, he set them on the drying rack and switched off the light.

Checking his watch, he knew Vivienne should be there in about five minutes, so he gently nudged Lillian's arm. She shook and opened her eyes.

"Well, hello, sleepy. I think you're about ready for a proper nap. Vivienne will be here any minute."

Somewhat disoriented, Lillian took a few seconds to show signs of coherence. Walter smiled when he saw the warmth return with a smile and a twinkle in her gaze.

There was a light knock at the door, and Walter peeped through the curtain on the side window.

"It's Viv. I'll be going. Are you going to be okay?" Walter hesitated.

"Yes. I'm quite fine. Thank you for coming and spending the afternoon. And especially for the delicious soup and cookies."

"You're welcome. Do you think we'll be seeing you at the pool soon?"

"I'm sure I'll be back to my old self in a couple of days. I'll see you there?" Lillian took his arm and squeezed.

"You betcha," Walter put his arms around her shoulders and gave her a gentle hug. When he opened the door, Vivienne had stepped back to the car and was waiting by the passenger front door. She assisted him in, and they both waved to Lillian as they pulled away.

"Good day?"

"Great day." Walter stared out the window.

When they got home, Walter had energy to burn. It felt like if he could lift a thousand pounds, well maybe even a hundred, he would. There was an actual *need* to do something. Shoveling the front walk should do the trick. Vivienne was tied up with clients on the phone, which distracted her enough for him to get started. He ambled out to the garage and found the large snow shovel. It felt a bit heavy, nothing unusual, considering he hadn't held a shovel in at least four years.

He began at the porch and shoveled toward the street. This was the proper way to do it, or at least it was his way.

He was about halfway through when he heard a loud shriek. He turned to see Vivienne in the doorway with a horrified look on her face.

"Oh my god, are you crazy! Put the shovel down. Now. I can't believe you're out here doing this. What the hell were you thinking?" Vivienne's face revved up from pale white to fire engine red in a matter of seconds.

"I'm fine. I needed to do *something*. I feel good. Don't worry. Go back in; I'm almost done." Walter turned his back and continued.

"You are done now." Vivienne stormed over and attempted to grab the shovel.

"Now look, Missy. I was trying to be nice. I know you're only acting like this because you worry. But get your damn hands off this damn shovel. I will be in when I say I am done. Not a minute less." Walter's hands trembled.

He wasn't sure if Vivienne finally understood how angry he was or if she just thought it would be best not to battle in the front yard. Whatever it was that motivated her, she stomped off and back into the house.

Walter took a breath and waited a few moments before resuming his preoccupation with the snow. He hadn't gotten that angry with Vivienne in a long time.

The last time was shortly after Gina had passed away. Once again, she was trying to help, and he understood that. But there was a difference between aiding someone and babying them. Vivienne often leaned toward the latter. It was in her nature to mother. She was caring and nurturing, but damn it, he was an adult.

When he finished to his satisfaction, he replaced the shovel in its spot in the garage and sat on the porch admiring his work. That was until the first snow flurry came. And then another and another. Walter couldn't do anything but let out a loud roar of laughter.

When he was inside and settled, he called Frank. He hadn't spoken to him since the funeral, and he thought it was time he checked up on him. The call was brief, but at least he knew Frank was still among the living. He knew his thoughts bordered on morose, but when someone like Frank, who had been married for so many years, loses their spouse—they shrivel up inside. He knew firsthand how that felt. When he lost Gina, he lost his will to breathe.

If his friends and family hadn't pushed him, he would have faded away. Before he hung up with Frank, he had asked him to meet at the pool in the morning. Frank was hesitant and didn't give a definitive answer, but Walter hoped for the best.

He sat in his recliner and turned on the news. The local first and then CBS Evening News with Scott Pelley. Much to Walters's dismay, he had read in the morning paper that Pelley was being replaced. Walter enjoyed the newscaster and vowed to switch channels if he didn't like the new guy or gal. For now, though, he settled in for half an hour of professionalism.

Vivienne meandered in quietly. She had a plate full of spaghetti with two meatballs and hot sausage. Walter knew the sausage was hot because Vivienne never added sweet Italian sausage to her gravy, a recipe that Gina had taught her. She set the plate on a TV tray, and beside it, placed a napkin and silverware. Disappearing into the kitchen, she reemerged a few seconds later with a glass of diet Pepsi. The only soda Walter liked to drink when consuming Italian food. For years Gina tried to get him to share a glass of red wine with her, but Walter could never get a taste for it. In fact, he didn't like wine, period. Give him a good scotch on the rocks or Jack Daniels bourbon, and he could hold his own.

The door swung open, and Robert came in shivering and covered in snow.

"Hi, Dad. Mmm. Dinner smells fantastic." Robert eyed Walter's plate. "How was your day?"

"Good."

Vivienne came in and greeted Robert with a kiss.

"I can't believe you made gravy today. It's perfect. You know it started snowing again." Robert hung up his coat.

"I can see that. How was work?"

"Same old, same old. Dad's not giving me anything. How was your day?"

"Fine. I drove him to Lillian's. He stayed there for a few hours." Vivienne glanced at Walter.

"Oh, that's good. He got out for a while. Hey. Did you have the neighbor kid shovel the walkway?"

"Not exactly. How can you tell? I thought it was snowing. Your coat is soaked."

"It's not completely covered yet. Wait—you said no. Did you do it?" Robert knitted his brows.

"I did," Walter chimed in.

"What the hell were you thinking?" Robert walked toward Walter, but Vivienne grabbed his hand.

"Don't. We've already gone down this road, and it didn't end well," Vivienne pleaded.

Walter set down his fork and looked up from the television. Robert caught his gaze and dropped the subject.

Dinner was every bit as good as Gina's, but given the shoveling debate, Walter would not offer any compliments to the cook. Instead, he quietly savored every bite until the plate was clean. Pushing away the tray table, Walter settled back for a night of his favorite comedy shows. *The Big Bang Theory* was his number-one favorite. He didn't always get the gaming references, but he loved the way Sheldon flaunted his self-appointed superiority. His second favorite show was *Mom*. Allison Janney cracked him up.

At ten o'clock, he was exhausted and decided to turn in. He needed a ride to the pool in the morning, but rather than soften the bad blood between him and Vivienne, he opted to call Norman. Walter knew he never missed a day at the pool.

Monday through Friday, like clockwork, Norman was there at eight a.m. sharp. He lived only two blocks away, and the man really was a good guy. Walter couldn't imagine he would refuse him a ride. He'd call him at first light.

There was a hesitation before going upstairs. The living room in the diminished evening light hid secrets that Walter carried in his heart. He could barely make out the frames of the family photos, but he knew exactly where to look for a particular one.

He reached out to the second shelf from the top of the bookcase and kissing the fingers of his other hand, he touched it gently. His cheeks puffed, and his jaw tightened. He pushed back the lump in his throat and swiped the end of his nose with his index finger. Turning to the staircase, he filled his lungs with oxygen and expelled it, relaxing his body. He felt each step with the pulsating ache that shot through his hips and knees. Tightly grabbing the railing, he used it for leverage to pull as he grew closer to the landing and the end of his upward challenge. His cane had been hooked around his left wrist, and he used it to steady himself on the walk to his bedroom.

After the routine he had become so accustomed to, he slipped into bed and under the covers. Pulling them up to his chin, he felt a chill creep up his spine. He wasn't cold. It was the bitterness of regret. He should have apologized to Vivienne. Told her he understood and let it be. Thanked her for a delicious meal and all the care and attention she gave him. *What the hell was wrong with me? Why did I continuously treat her with such disdain? She is the boy's mother. How could she function? He asked himself every day. Then why, Walter, do you do this?* He flipped his pillow to hide the wet spot. Closing his eye, the last thing in his mind's eye were flashes of *him*. This would be a hard night.

Chapter Twelve

Walter was right. Norman was more than happy to pick him up. In fact, he sounded ecstatic. The two men had decided to leave a half hour early and stop for bagels and coffee on the way. Walter was especially glad about this because he didn't have to converse with Vivienne or eat a breakfast she had prepared. Instead, he left a note next to the coffee pot informing her of his whereabouts and breakfast plans.

Walter felt good knocking around stories of the old days. First, there was lunch with Vincent, then Lillian and Norman. Each one had their own spin on the past, and for Walter, it was more than entertaining. It was remembering a life that he had and loved. The best times on this planet were behind him.

After they had finished their last drop of coffee, they continued on to their aquatic mission. When they arrived, the parking lot was fairly crowded, and Walter huffed. He knew this meant fighting the low end for space with the toddlers. Not that they weren't cute to watch, but they splashed—a lot.

He was pleasantly surprised to find out that the reason it had been so crowded was not because of a tribe of youngsters, but rather, it was senior day. No one under the age of sixty-five was allowed admission for the entire day. Norman grinned and gave Walter a thumbs-up when they found out the news.

Norman aimed straight for the water while Walter stood and got the lay of the land. The usual suspects were there. Harry and Evelyn were wading near the edge with Frank beside them. Tony Trash was busy bothering the ladies' exercise group, and Adolfo was busy trying to fend them off. Only one person was missing—the most important one. Walter's heart sank.

He was almost positive she would have come. He knew she hadn't felt one hundred percent, but he had hoped their conversation yesterday would put some life back into her soul.

"Looking for someone?" A soft voice echoed from behind him.

Walter smiled and turned his head to look over his right shoulder. There she was.

"Good morning, old girl." Walter tipped his imaginary hat.

"Who you calling old? You old coot." Lillian grinned.

"Would you like to go into the pool?" Walter put out a bent arm.

"I should say I do." Lillian wrapped her arm around his.

The two of them sauntered to the steps and steadily descended into the pool with a firm grip on the grab bars. Once in, they glided through the familiar and intoxicating scent of chlorine and body lotion. Most of the seniors were sensitive to the chemicals and often lathered up in moisturizer with the notion it would let the water slide off and keep the chemicals from damaging their skin. Walter always chuckled when he heard this theory. They weren't considering that half of their bodies were submerged in the chemical soup the entire time they were in the pool.

Lillian pointed to the corner of the pool that was less crowded. It was in the five-foot area near the built-in ladder. She was barely over five feet but could stand if she stayed close to the pool wall. She told Walter she preferred the ambiance. Walter shook his head; the entire pool area looked the same to him.

They had been hanging out in their private cubby for about ten minutes when Frank glided up. He was a swimmer in his youth and could still paddle through the water with elegance.

"Lillian. So nice to see you back." Frank leaned against the pool wall.

"You too. I'm so sorry about Elsa. I wish I could have attended the funeral, but I was not feeling well. How are you doing?"

"Well, thank you for that. I know you had a rough go of it. She knows too. I'm doing what I'm doing. It's too quiet without her. I think of her every minute of every day." Frank looked toward the wall of windows.

"How are you today, Walter?" Frank backhanded Walter's shoulder.

"Today I'm good, Frank. I'm happy to see you came." Walter grinned.

"Me too, buddy. Me too."

The time passed quickly with his good friends, and Walter surprisingly enjoyed every minute. He felt like he had made a difference in their day. At home, he was usually the burden, but today, he was the strong shoulder. He'd never admit it to Ryan, but the kid had a great idea when he suggested Walter join the program. Some of these people really needed him.

Norman dropped him off at the front door around three o'clock. They had spent six hours hanging out at the pool. Walter couldn't believe how late it was. When he walked in, Vivienne had her calculator on the dining room table with a stack of bills. Many of them were Walter's; he knew it. Robert and Viv only had the utilities and mortgage.

Neither one of them had any significant health issues, and he could see by the logos on the envelopes they were from the hospital.

He had been in the hospital for twenty-seven days after the incident, hooked up to a spaghetti mess of wires, tubes, and machines. The cost after insurance was being absorbed by his children.

Living on a fixed income, Walter was stretched as far as his budget would go. His three sons got together and agreed to split the balance amongst each of them. The burning in the pit of his stomach was matched by the rush of blood to his head. Walter picked up one of the opened envelopes and slipped out the bill.

Vivienne shook her head and reached for it, but it was too late. He squinted his eyes to focus. He had left his damn glasses in his coat pocket. Adjusting the paper so it became clearer, he focused on the bottom figure—$12,752.00.

Walter looked up and met Vivienne's watery eyes. He knew why she was upset, and very little had to do with the bill. Every time one of them came, they were a reminder of that day. Walter sat down next to her and reached out. Vivienne leaned in, laid her head on his shoulder, and hugged him. Walter's shirt was damp with tears, so he squeezed her even tighter. When she finally pulled away, he handed her his hanky from his pocket. She wiped her eyes and cheeks and then kissed him on the forehead. Not a word was spoken about the argument the day before. They both understood the pain.

Dinner was good, a hearty beef stew. Walter enjoyed every bite. *I love dinner*, he thought. Then he laughed to himself. Who was he kidding? He loved food. His growing belly was evidence of that.

He had been svelte for much of his life, but when he hit seventy, he decided it was time to throw caution to the wind. He didn't just throw it; he catapulted it straight into the abyss. All the foods Gina tried to steer him away from became fair game—chocolate anything and fried, the greasier the better. Soda, ice cream by the pint, and cookies from the bakery. And let us not forget when Vivienne baked. The girl made the best apple pie on the planet. Gina would be horrified by his diet. Robert and Viv tried to control his garbage consumption, but they were unsuccessful, and Walter figured they finally just gave up.

He was just settling in on his recliner when the phone rang. He could hear Robert's voice but not make out what he was saying. A moment later, he came into the living room and handed Walter the phone.

"It's Lillian Grainger." Robert's cheeks puckered.

"Oh. Is everything alright?" Walter scooted forward.

"She sounds fine." Robert went back to the kitchen. "Hello." Walter's chest tightened.

"Hello, Walter. I wanted to thank you for such a lovely day at the pool. Will you be there tomorrow?"

"Uh. Sure. Yes, I'll definitely be there. Nine o'clock?" Walter cleared his throat.

"Lovely. I'll see you then. I'll bring some snacks too. Do you like chocolate chip cookies and Ritz crackers?"

"Yes. They're both good."

"Perfect. See you tomorrow."

Walter hit the off button on the phone and set it down on the side table. Robert came in on his way upstairs and took the phone.

"So, do you have a ... date?" Robert smirked.

"What? No. Lillian is my dear friend. I'm helping her through a rough patch. That's all. I'm married to your mother."

"Mom's been gone for four years now. I know she'd want you to be happy."

"Well, I am, and it's not a date." Walter scowled.

"Whatever you say."

Robert whistled the song L-O-V-E by Louis Armstrong the entire way upstairs.

Walter grumbled and went back to searching for a show he could use to fill the next two hours. There was a marathon of Jesse Stone movies on channel three hundred and ten. Walter was thrilled. Jesse Stone was a city cop who moved to a small town and became sheriff. Tom Selleck played Jesse. He was one of Walter's all-time favorite actors.

Walter made it through all the first movie and about half the second before dozing off into a deep REM sleep. Once again, he was a prisoner to the cruel motion picture featured nightly in his dreams.

His eyes fluttered, and his fists hit the air.

"You're a coward. I won't give you the pleasure of closing my eyes. Go to hell. I'm sure they're waiting for you."

The sound of his own voice startled Walter, and he jolted awake. The second movie was ending, and he looked around the room. The lights were off except for the one on the side of his chair. Vivienne and Robert had gone to bed.

He grabbed the remote and shut the television. He wasn't sure of the time; the numbers on the cable box were fuzzy. But he wanted to be fresh in the morning for his day at the pool, so he mustered the strength to go upstairs to bed.

Just before he got into bed, he kissed a picture of Gina. It was a black and white in a 5x7 antique silver frame on the top of his bureau. She was about forty when he took the picture. She had been sitting at the kitchen table gazing out the window. She hadn't even realized he had the camera. She looked so beautiful. Her shoulder-length hair was softly pulled back, and she wore no makeup. He had never met another woman who stirred his heart quite like she did.

After he had taken the picture, the noise startled her, and she chased him out of the kitchen. He didn't know it at the time, but it would be his favorite photo of her for the rest of their lives together.

He opened the window slightly to let a little fresh air in. The heat always dried out his sinuses, and he didn't want a stuffy head in the morning. He had brought up his usual half glass of water and took a sip before setting it down on the nightstand. Sleep was overtaking his body, weighing it down and sinking him into the mattress below. His mind slowly grew blank, and he welcomed the dark of nothingness. He saw no horror that night, only the sweet face of little Lillian Grainger bringing him Ritz crackers.

Walter shivered and pulled the covers up to his chin. He hated this drawback of cracking the window open. The room was somewhere between night and day. Walter fumbled with the little alarm clock on the side of his bed. The dial was illuminated to reveal that it was six-thirty a.m. He had slept like a rock for a solid six hours.

He felt wonderful. Throwing the covers off, he grabbed his cane and went to the window to shut it. Then he crawled back into bed. He wanted to enjoy the sunrise from under the warmth of his cozy comforter. The golden hue of rays started in the far corner of his bedroom near the closet door and slowly crept up, drenching the entire room in a bright, birds-singing, life's-gonna-be-good kind of day.

He had left a note on the kitchen table for Vivienne. After their exchange yesterday, he knew it was back to business as usual, and he needed a ride to the pool. He showered, put on his bathing suit, and dressed. Grabbing his bag packed with boxers and a sweatshirt, he moseyed downstairs for breakfast. Yep, business as usual. Vivienne was taking out a plate of pancakes and sausage from the oven. She often cooked and then placed his plate into the oven to keep it warm until he came downstairs.

"Looks delicious, thank you." Walter sat down.

Vivienne looked sideways at Robert, who had the same befuddled expression. Walter caught the whole thing.

"Stop, you two. Can't I have a happy morning once in a while?"

"Yes. Of course. We're happy to see you well ... happy." Vivienne filled his cup with coffee.

Vivienne set the pot down and grabbed her stomach before racing into the hall bathroom.

"Is she okay?" Walter asked Robert.

"Yeah, she's good. Just a touch of the stomach flu. She has a doctor's appointment tomorrow morning. It's going around. I had several people at work call out sick over the past week."

"If she doesn't feel well, I can ask Norman to pick me up. I'm sure he wouldn't mind. He has to pass us up to get to the pool."

"Nonsense. I'm fine," Vivienne came back into the room. "It's really a mild case. I can drive you. There's no problem."

"Okay. If you're sure you're alright."

"I am." Vivienne grabbed a cup of coffee and sat down.

"Listen, boys. I've been thinking. We should go out to dinner tonight. I would like to eat something I haven't cooked in the past two weeks."

Robert looked up from his phone. "Uh, sure, Babe. Anywhere in mind?"

"Yes. I have been craving Chinese food all week. How about we go to The Golden Flower on 3rd street?"

Both Walter and Robert nodded their heads in agreement. A lesson they both learned from Gina. When the cook says, let's eat out... you eat out.

Vivienne was quiet on the car ride over to the pool. Walter gazed at her; she was a bit pale. He didn't want to agitate her, so he kept his thoughts to himself.

In contrast to the day before, the parking lot was empty. Walter saw Lillian's car parked in the front row along with Norman's and Tony Trash's. Walter had hoped Tony wouldn't show up. He had no information to lead him to believe he wouldn't, just his wishful thinking. He asked Vivienne to pick him up at three o'clock if she didn't hear from him sooner.

Vivienne smiled and drove off to meet her mom for coffee and pastries at their favorite French bakery.

Walter checked in, placed his belongings in a locker, and gingerly walked out to the low end of the pool. Lillian was sitting at the top step holding the railing with one hand and gliding through the water with the other. She was beaming.

"Oh, there you are. I thought maybe one of these old dogs had beaten me to the punch." Walter grinned.

"The only old dog here is you." Lillian splashed him lightly.

Tony Trash waded over, and Lillian greeted him with a lively hello. Walter couldn't understand how she could be so nice to him all the time. Yes, he did have a rough break in life, but everyone has their secrets. It doesn't mean you get a pass on manners.

"Good morning Lillian. Oh, and you too, Walter. Does the water feel cold to you today? I'm freezing," Tony crossed his arms and shivered.

"No. The pool is warm. Tony, are you feeling okay today?" Lillian sounded concerned.

Walter just ignored him.

"I do feel achy, but I thought it was because I stayed in the pool too long yesterday." Tony gingerly sat on the step below them.

"Maybe you should get out and lie on one of the chaise lounges. Is there anything I can do?" Lillian patted Tony's forearm.

"No. Thank you, you're very kind. I think I will go and lay down, though." Tony slowly got up.

Walter almost fell off the step. Tony had been so gracious to Lillian. Maybe he really was sick.

"The poor man is all alone. I feel sorry for him." Lillian glanced over at Tony as he was reclining in the chase.

"How could you possibly feel sorry for such a scoundrel? He is nothing but insulting to just about every woman who comes in contact with him. In fact, you're the only one that I've heard him speak so kindly to."

"Not true," Lillian argued.

"Oh, really. Who else has he been a human to?" Walter sounded snarky.

"Gina. He never said anything out of the way to Gina."

Walter turned away. She was right. Tony was always a gentleman to his beloved girl.

They were both startled by an ear-piercing scream. Walter scanned the room, searching for the source. There was a commotion near the chase lounges, and Ryan was standing over Tony Trash, pumping his chest. Evelyn and Harry were beside him, and Evelyn was wailing. Walter and Lillian quickly stepped out of the pool and grabbed their towels. Ryan wouldn't give up. He kept pumping even after the paramedics arrived. They worked on him for several minutes but couldn't regain a heartbeat. Tony was pronounced dead at ten thirty-two a.m.

Walter and Lillian sat down next to the lifeless body. His eyes were closed, and his face held the vacancy of death. Ryan had tried unsuccessfully to instruct them to go back to the pool. They were waiting for the coroner, and neither wanted to leave his side.

Walter couldn't understand why it was so important to stay with this man who annoyed him most of his adult life, but he couldn't bring himself to get up.

Walter patted Lillian's hand, and she clasped his tightly. The two friends sat in silence until the body was wheeled out. Lillian began sobbing, and Walter hugged her. Drawing her close, he tried to soothe her with soft whispers of words stating the usual, *he's in a better place.* But Walter wasn't so sure he believed it. They just always sounded right at the time.

He walked Lillian to the women's locker room and went into his to change. When they were both dressed, they met in the lobby. Walter had called Vivienne and told her what had happened. They were going to the diner, and Lillian would bring him home later.

It was chilly outside, and Lillian put the heat on in the car.

"I think I would like a hot bowl of soup and some

coffee." Lillian shivered.

"That sounds good to me. I'm not very hungry." Walter fixed the vent to point away.

"Is it too warm in here for you? I can lower the heat?" Lillian inquired.

"No, it's fine. I just don't like it blowing directly on me. But it feels good. The chill went straight to my bones when we left the building."

"Mine too. Honestly, it bothers me more each year. Either it's getting colder, or after seventy-five, your body can't take the extreme weather."

"Sorry to say, Lillian dear, but I think it's our age," Walter softly chuckled.

"I know you're right, but sometimes it's better to make excuses." Lillian turned on the left blinker. "Easier on my ego," she whispered.

When they arrived at the diner, it was empty. Walter was happy. He didn't like dealing with the loud noise on a good day, and today it would have been worse. He yearned for the calm.

They requested a booth, and as luck would have it, the hostess walked them to the back of the restaurant. Walter thought it odd, being it was pretty much empty, but he didn't complain. He was happy to be removed from the main dining area.

The waitress approached the table with a small pad and pen in hand. Her hair was pulled back in a tight blonde bun, and she wore very little makeup. Walter thought she was probably older than she looked because, up close, he could see the fine lines of laughter caressing the outer corners of her eyes.

"Hi. My name is Sherry, and I'll be your server today. Here are a couple of menus. Can I start you off with some drinks?" Sherry waited for a response.

Walter nodded to Lillian to go first.

"Thank you. I'll have coffee with cream and no sugar, please."

"I'll have the same, thank you." Walter averted his eyes back to the menu.

Sherry left and returned a few minutes later with two coffees, a stainless-steel creamer, and two ice waters. She carefully set them down and then placed extra napkins at the end of the table.

"Have you decided on your order?" Sherry stood poised with the pen, ready to write.

Lillian ordered a bowl of clam chowder, and Walter's eyes lit up. He hadn't seen that on the menu.

"I'll have the same. Do you have oyster crackers?" Walter put some cream into his coffee.

"We do."

Lillian put her hand up. "Could I have some, too, please? That sounds good."

"Certainly."

Sherry took the menus from them and scurried off behind the counter to the kitchen.

"That was a great suggestion, Walter. I don't know why I didn't think of the oyster crackers. I love them." Lillian placed her napkin on her lap.

"I don't think either of us is in a thinking mood today." Walter furrowed his brow.

"True. I can't believe he's gone. One minute chatting in his usual Tony Trash fashion, and the next—he looked so different. Dare I say, I'll miss him." Lillian's eyes teared up.

"Strange how that happens. Tony always drove me nuts, but I can't shake this sadness. I tried to avoid him all the time, and now the thought of never hearing his agitating rhetoric…"

"I know. You were hard on him, but he was that kind of guy. He was never able to get over the misfortunes that life had placed in his path. He held deep grudges, and it made him bitter. I wish you could have known him before. He was a great fella." Lillian sipped her coffee.

"Well, maybe I still can."

"What do you mean?"

"Tell me about him. Tell me what he was like before he became Tony Trash."

"Okay then." Lillian tilted her head and smiled.

Sherry brought their soup and oyster crackers and refilled their coffee. The two sat for the next hour and a half while Lillian brought all her fond memories of Tony to life. Walter listened intently. He had heard the hardships of the man's life from Vincent but not the human side. Lillian knew him better than Walter had thought.

They had practically grown up together like brother and sister. Their mothers had been close, and the kids saw each other practically every day. Lillian had never had any romantic notions for Tony, and as far as she knew, he had none for her. But they had built a solid friendship and were there for each other through the years.

Walter found himself submerged in the personality of a man he never knew. His sadness compounded. *If he had only spent time with him.*

"You can't do that," Lillian cautioned.

"Do what?" Walter was confused.

"I see that glaze in your eyes. You're asking yourself the *what if* question. There was no way for you to know his past. It was his to share, and if he chose not to, then that was up to him. He had turned into a mean-spirited soul, and that is who you knew. You can't rewrite history and change anything, so stop it."

"Wow. Aren't you the smart one, Missy." Walter wiped his brow with the napkin.

"I am... and don't ever forget it. You alright? Warm?"

"Yeah. I think they have the heat turned up to tropical in here." Walter took a sip of water.

"You ready to break out of this joint?" Lillian scooted to the end of the booth.

"Yup," Walter took out a five-dollar bill and placed it under his coffee cup.

When they got to the register, Lillian tried to grab the bill, but Walter was too quick. He tipped his imaginary hat to her and handed the cashier a twenty. Lillian waved and turned to walk toward the front door.

The chill had officially elevated to *downright cold,* and the two quickly got into the car and once again blasted the heat.

"This weather is like a yo-yo. First, it's cold, then it's warm, then cold, and now it's warm again. Maybe Tony is the lucky one."

"Walter Reilly, never say that again," Lillian's tone was sharp.

"I'm sorry. Poor taste," Walter said apologetically.

Walter beat himself up mentally the entire ride home. He knew his words stung. The last thing he wanted to do was hurt Lillian.

She dropped him off at the front of the house with promises to meet at the pool in a few days. Neither had the desire to go back just yet. Lillian would call Tony's family and see what their intentions were for the funeral. When she found out some information, she would let Walter know. He thanked her and waved as she pulled away. He stood alone for a second, surveying the neighborhood. Nothing would ever be as it was. He moaned a soft whine of sadness before collecting himself. Vivienne would surely be at the door as soon as he stepped foot inside, and he needed to prepare for the barrage of questions. All he really wanted to do was go lay down and forget the morning.

Chapter Thirteen

The next few days were sedate. Walter stayed home mostly watching reruns of Gunsmoke, Bonanza, and Colombo. Vivienne had some family come in from out of town, and she was busy running all over and sightseeing all those places that people think you spend your off time doing when you're a native of the city. Walter was thankful for the quiet. Robert had offered to come home and take him out to lunch a day or two during the week, but Walter declined. He had gone to his "wallow place."

For most people, the word wallow signified an expression of a place in yourself built on sadness and loneliness. But for Walter, it was much different. Sure, he had those days where he had to dig himself out of the hole and lift himself up, but this wasn't like that. On the days he chose as his "wallow place," it was his time to forget. Not to focus on the losses in his life, but to have straight-out, no-nonsense, fully committed TV time. He would wallow in the shows that he enjoyed the most. What better way to block out the painful and hardest parts of his life. Maybe the word wallow wasn't correct, but that's what he labeled it, and it worked for him.

The house was vacant, and his recliner and three hundred channels were his own for the better part of the week. He wasn't going to waste a minute of being king of his island. Microwave lunches, sweets when he wanted, and a warm flannel blanket completed his reign.

Three days went by without a word from Lillian. She had said she'd call when the funeral arrangements were made, so he waited. On the fourth day, the phone rang, and it was the call he had been waiting for. Tony was going to be buried on Saturday.

There wouldn't be the usual viewing like they had for Elsa. The family either did not approve or didn't care. Whatever the reason, the three-day ritual was waived.

Lillian had offered to pick up Walter, and they could attend the services together. He had suggested they go with Vincent, who had volunteered to taxi them for the day. Lillian thanked him and agreed it would be best. Walter had a day and a half left to enjoy his television stupor. He would make the most of it. After a quick lunch of microwaveable personal pan pizza, he decided to make a hot fudge sundae. Not skimping on any of the ingredients, he scooped in a healthy portion of pistachio ice cream before loading on the extra nuts, rainbow sprinkles, hot fudge, and caramel sauce with a mound of whipped cream and three maraschino cherries to top it off. He was about to take his first bite when, as fate would have it, Vivienne came home.

Her eyes widened as she glared at the delectable tower of sweets in his bowl. She started to walk toward him, but something stopped her. Walter watched as if an invisible rope had tied itself around her waist and tugged her back. She abruptly turned around and went upstairs.

He never found out what angel had decided to shine on him that day and grant him reprieve from the wraith of Vivienne Reilly, but he didn't question it. He just sat back and let the full blend of six heavenly elements whisk his taste buds off to nirvana.

After an uneasy night of tossing and turning, Walter woke up Saturday morning with a weight looming over his soul. Today he would go and honor a man for which he held no honor. A man who could bring him to the brink of unrest and yet also fill him with a magnitude of regret.

He would say goodbye to him one last time, all the while hoping for a reprieve from the finality of death.

Vincent picked him up at eleven a. m. sharp, and they went to Lillian's. When they got there, Walter walked up to the front door and escorted her to the car. She insisted on sitting in the back seat, and he didn't push the issue. They were solemn on the drive to the church. Walter had nothing to say, and apparently, neither did Lillian or Vincent. When they arrived, there were two black limousines and a hearse parked out front. Walter assumed the limos were for family. He knew who the hearse was for.

The Mass was long but memorable. For the first time in a long time, Walter soaked in the singing from the choir and the priest's words. They moved him in a way he hadn't felt for a long time. The trip to the burial plot was a short drive. Not many had gathered. Walter figured most of the congregation had gone on to the restaurant the family booked for the after-service gathering. The priest kept his words short, and they were back in the car in about forty-five minutes.

"It was a lovely service," Lillian was barely audible from the back seat.

Neither Walter nor Vincent said a word. They just let Lillian's words stand alone.

Walter would have liked to say something heartwarming, but nothing came. Not even a simple yes could pass through his lips. He had no idea why this was so difficult.

When they got to the restaurant, it was crowded. They took a seat at the furthest table away from the family. They felt it would be best if those closest to them occupied the nearby tables. Walter had suggested to Lillian that it would be okay to leave him and Vincent if she would rather sit with the family, but she dismissed the notion.

It was buffet style, and Walter carried his plate straight to the roast beef. A gentleman was slicing it fresh off the rump.

It was medium-rare, just the way Walter loved it, especially since it was so difficult to get red meat prepared that way in a restaurant in today's day and age. Now that the world was keen on the health risks of undercooked meat, medium-well was the rarest for most establishments.

After receiving two large slices, he moseyed over to the mashed potatoes and gravy. Surveying the green beans, he chose to pass on a vegetable. He did enjoy salad and figured it would count to balance out his meat and potatoes. He heaped several scoops of ranch dressing onto the crisp green leaves trimmed with cucumbers, onions, and tomatoes. He was set. When he returned to the table, Lillian and Vincent were scooting in with a plate of food in front of them. Lillian's plate was scarcely covered.

The server brought each of them water and asked what drink they would like. Almost in unison they replied, *coffee.*

Lunch was somber. Neither struggled to make small talk, and Walter could breathe easier knowing that he didn't have to try and keep up.

Tony's eldest sister stood up at one point and gave a toast to her baby brother. She shared a few fond childhood memories and professed how much he would be missed. Dabbing her eyes and cheeks with a tissue when she was done, her frail body shook as she held onto the tabletop and sat down. The room resumed its quiet lull of conversation until the first guest to gain the courage to make an exit got up. The rest of the guests soon followed. Within minutes the area was cleaned out.

"Well, I guess that's our cue to leave." Walter placed his napkin on the table.

Lillian and Vincent nodded.

As they pulled up to Lillian's home, she thanked them for the ride and promised to call Walter later on in the day so they could make plans to go to the pool during the week.

Walter watched her dwindling shape enter the house. She appeared exceptionally small to him. He hadn't noticed it earlier, but he swore she was getting thinner than she had ever been.

"Vincent, did Lillian look okay to you?" Walter turned his head toward him.

"Well, given the day, I'd say she looked just fine."

"You're probably right."

Walter dropped it even though he thought Vincent was wrong. It had been a rough day, but her delicate frame was shrinking; he wasn't imagining it.

Vincent pulled up to the driveway this time so Walter wouldn't have far to walk. He thanked his friend and quickly shuffled to the front door. The temperature had dropped, and all he could think about was the warmth of his house and coziness of his recliner.

Vivienne greeted him at the door. "Hi, Dad. You okay?"

"I am. Viv, could I ask a favor?" Walter hung up his coat.

"Sure." Vivienne walked into the living room and sat on the sofa.

Walter followed and settled beside her.

"I'm very worried about Lillian. She's ill. It's bad... bone cancer. She hasn't said a word to me about this. She's going for treatment, but I think it's knocking the life right out of her. I'm not sure it's working. When Gina got ill, she did lose weight from the treatment, but Lillian is withering, and I'm not so sure she's going to get through it."

"How did you find out if Lillian hasn't told you?" Vivienne's brows raised.

"Ryan. He made me promise not to say anything to her," Walter coughed.

"I'm so sorry. What do you need me to do?"

"I don't want to upset her, but maybe the next time you drop me off at the pool, you can come and speak with her. She might tell you what's going on, and you can find out about her treatment."

"Are you sure? This could work, or go horribly wrong if she thinks I'm prying." Vivienne bit her lip.

"I would appreciate it. Hey, speaking about the doctor, how did your visit go? Did they say anything?"

"No. I have to wait for the test results to come back. But don't worry. It's nothing. I'm probably not eating right. I've been racing around lately and grabbing too much to-go food. I'm sure it will be something ridiculous like that." Vivienne patted Walter's knee and then got up. "When are you meeting at the pool?"

"We need to confirm, but I think maybe on Tuesday."

"Okay. Let me know, and we can put our plan into action." She grinned.

"Thank you. I really do appreciate this."

"I know you do." Vivienne grabbed her coat. "I'm running up to the store. You need anything?"

"Will you pick up some of those little bakery cookies I like? You know, the ones with the cherry in the center."

"You got it. I'll be home shortly."

After Vivienne left, Walter went up to his room to change out of his suit. He put on a pair of flannel lounge pants and a long sleeve t-shirt. Time to get lost in a marathon of *Criminal Minds*. Every day of the week, channel fifty-one aired continuous episodes from four to seven p.m. Redundancy had a way of easing Walter's stress.

A loud boom from the front door startled Walter, waking him from a very rare peaceful sleep. Vivienne removed her coat before placing a small pink box in his lap on the way to the kitchen. Like a child finding the golden ticket, Walter's pulse raced as he lifted the lid to the sugary treasure. Taking the first bite sent an explosion of bliss to his taste buds. The cookie melted ever so gently into his mouth, and he closed his eyes to enjoy the euphoria.

His happiness trance was abruptly interrupted when Vivienne returned to the room.

"Don't eat that whole box. Your sugar will go sky-high. Just a few, and we'll put the rest away for the week."

"Listen, I thank you for picking them up, but I'm not five. I don't need you to tell me what I should do. Give me some credit, will you?" Walter huffed. She had ruined his pastry experience.

Vivienne went to say something and then abruptly shut her mouth and turned around. She was mumbling something to herself about being ungrateful as she slammed the door to the kitchen.

Walter didn't care. He had his cookies.

Halfway through his crime marathon, Walter reached into the pink box and had to shuffle his hand around to grab a cookie. He looked down and nearly dropped the box. He had eaten three-quarters of its contents. If Vivienne saw this, she would explode. Especially after his stance on his willpower. He closed the lid and set the box between his left hip and the chair. He didn't want her coming in and picking it up. Later he would take it to his room. His stomach began churning, and the calm waters were replaced with a wave of choppy tides. He grabbed his gut and took in a breath, hoping to hold off the inevitable. It didn't work. Within five minutes, he was dashing toward the bathroom.

When he finished, his stomach felt better, but he had missed the entire episode he had been watching. Adding to the misery was the disappearance of the little pink box that was no longer on his chair. Instead, there was a small white piece of paper.

Walter hesitantly walked over and picked it up. As he unfolded the message, he was flooded with both curiosity and dread. He knew who the author of the correspondence was. There were, after all, only two of them in the house. Adjusting his glasses to focus, the paper contained two simple words: THE END. Walter sat down and reflected. Confusion clouded his thoughts, *THE END of the box? Did she throw them out? Wasn't she picking them up from the bakery anymore? I swear that girl can be ridiculous at times. I'm not playing her game.*

Walter decided he would not give her the satisfaction of inquiring. But it didn't matter because a moment later, Vivienne stood in the doorway to the kitchen with a flattened pink box.

"Dad, I swear. You know how sick they can make you. I try to make things easier by indulging you in your sweet habit, but you know you need to have a little at a time. You already have diabetes. Do you want to have to take a shot every day? What's worse is I'm the stupid one. I think I'm being nice, but I'm actually the one giving you the sword."

Walter lost it. He knew what he had done. He didn't need a *mommy* scolding him.

"Who the hell do you think you are? We've gone around and around with this crap. I am not your child. If I want to consume an entire bakery of cookies, it is my choice. I know I ate too much. It was an accident. You don't need to remind me; the thirty minutes in the bathroom did that. Stop butting into my life. You don't want to pick up cookies for me, fine. We'll make this THE END, as your note so clearly pointed out. I'll get them myself when I go into town with Vincent," Walter snapped.

"Whatever you want. Get your own from now on." Vivienne had tears in her eyes.

Walter didn't care. He was going for the jugular. "And forget what I asked about Lillian. I'll deal with it on my own. I don't need your help. Just stop meddling into my life. You are Robert's wife; worry about him. You're not even my daughter."

Walter heard the last five words leave his lips but couldn't stop himself. It was too late. He wielded the blade and stabbed it right into Vivienne's heart.

His temper erupted, eradicating the compassion in him and obliterating his soft side. His patience this last year had been thin, but especially with Vivienne. He spoke his piece and wanted nothing more to do with her.

Interrupting their war, Robert came barreling through the front door. His wide grin quickly turned to a frown. Walter glared at his son while his gaze ping-ponged from his father to his wife.

"What now?" Robert's jaw tensed. Vivienne burst into a river of tears and ran upstairs.

Walter simply sat down and resumed his show.

Robert grabbed the remote and shut down the distraction.

"I've had it with you, dad. Vivienne tries over and over to make life a little easier for you. And no matter how many times we have this discussion, you always do it to her again and again. What in God's name is wrong with you? Why do you target the one person who is suffering beyond comprehension? Do you think you have some monopoly when it comes to grief? Or are you just that cold of a bastard? You are my father, but she is my wife. If this happens again, we will find you another place to live. Maybe one of my brothers will take you in."

Robert went upstairs to console his wife. Walter was stunned. His son had never been so disrespectful to him. He got up and yanked the newspaper off the dining room table and a pen from the hutch drawer. Sitting back in his recliner, he opened the paper to apartment rentals and began circling his prospects. Tomorrow he would regain his independence.

When Walter woke up Tuesday morning, the sun hadn't risen, and his room was still filled with the shadows of the night. He glanced at the illuminated clock on his bedside table, five a.m.

He lay in bed reflecting on what had happened a few days ago. His fight with Vivienne had opened a void of further interaction with her and very little with Robert. The house had become like a mausoleum. The only voices Walter heard during the day were the ones fighting crime or riding the range. His television had become an even closer companion than before.

Vincent was going to pick him up at 8 o'clock so they could go into the diner for a little bite before meeting Lillian at the pool. Vivienne no longer had his breakfast waiting for him. In fact, she didn't single out any meals for him over the past few days. His usual treats were his to come by, his dinner was served up by his own hands, and his dishes were also his responsibility. She had stopped his care other than meal preparation. Walter figured his eating was only a benefit because she cooked for Robert and herself. Otherwise, he was sure he would have been doing that too.

When he and Vincent got to the pool, a crowd of seniors gathered around Ryan and Grace in the lounge area.

No one was in the pool except for the tots in their beginners' swim class. Ryan was holding up a red flag and Grace, a blue one. The closer they got, Walter caught a few words; competition and prize. His stomach shot acid into the back of his throat. He was looking forward to a relaxing conversation with Lillian.

He needed to bask in the warmth of her friendship, *and* he was concerned for her health. But it didn't look like he was going to get either one of them.

It was Senior Game Day— a bunch of people running around like they were chasing their ever-so-elusive youth as it taunted them into exhaustion.. The mere mention of the words was enough for Walter to take a long walk off a short pier. He hated the stupidity of competition at any age over sixty.

He was unwillingly picked for the same team as Lillian, Adolfo, Harry, Norman, and some fellow he barely knew they called Polish Pete. Not because he was Polish but because he loved Polish sausage and apparently ate it all the time. Evelyn, Harry's wife, was excused from competition because of her slow-paced recovery. She had been hit by a drunk driver in the intersection downtown by a man who had a seizure behind the wheel. He t-boned her Cadillac, and they needed the Jaws of Life to extract her from the car. She was getting much better, but she wasn't anywhere near participating. Their team leader was Grace. A sweet girl whom Walter knew slightly from seeing her hang out on the front porch with Ryan. The game was fairly simple. First up, each team held a small brightly colored stick. Theirs was green like the slime his grandson used to laugh at on one of his Saturday morning cartoons. The idea was that each member had to walk the width of the low end of the pool and then hand off the stick to the next team member. Whichever side completed first would win.

The prize: coupons for a free pizza at Joey's Pies and Heroes.

The first one up for their team was Polish Pete. Walter had no idea if the man still retained any kind of agility that could aid in their chances of gaining a free lunch or dinner, but he was amazed when after the whistle blew, Pete took off like a speed demon. Forget the doubt; he pushed through the liquid barrier as if gliding on top of the water. His precision and ease made him finish minutes before the competition, and he handed the stick over to Norman.

Norman was painful to watch. He struggled, plowing through the water as if it were a vat of wet cement quickly drying with each step. The other team member had completed his lap and handed over the stick to an eagerly awaiting seventy-something before Norman had made it one journey across. Harry kept yelling at him to hurry up. The saddest part of this tournament of virility was that it appeared that he was giving it his best effort. His face was contorted, eyes squinting so drastically they looked like two slits in his head. The tension was apparent. When Norman finally reached their base and handed off the stick to Harry, his breath was shallow. Grace intervened and had him sit out while she cautiously kept an eye on him. *Oh please, we don't need a repeat of Tony Trash*, thought Walter.

After several minutes of calming down, Norman's breathing was more relaxed. Grace let him back in to join them but with the warning of no extreme physical activity. Norman grinned. He knew he had taken double everyone's time, but he voiced to Walter that he was elated that he had finished his lap. He had thought about halfway through, he was going to have to give up, but then he thought of Tony.

"The son of bitch would have loved this," he whispered to Walter. "Any chance to make us look bad."

Walter nodded and grinned.

When the day was over, Ryan's team had beaten them. They all shook hands, and Lillian graciously congratulated each one individually.

"All of you were awesome!" Ryan clapped.

"Grace and I had so much fun. I think we'll do this again next month," Ryan cheered.

"Wait a minute. We're not making a habit of these shenanigans. You almost killed poor Norman, for Christ's sake."

Everyone darted their eyes to Polish Pete.

"This was fun, yes. But just about everyone here had some kind of issue. Give us a break; you know we're older than dirt. You two kids mean well, but I think you're putting too much pressure on us. Joining the pool was supposed to be about getting some light exercise and some socializing. Not a one-way ticket to a pine box." Pete shook his head in disappointment.

For the first time in forever, Walter was happy he wasn't the one being a grump. Although he agreed with Pete and thought the whole day was a waste and a possible health hazard, at least he didn't have all eyes on him. He decided to keep his yap shut and let Pete take the floor and the noose if need be.

"Who agrees with me?" Pete waited.

Crap. He hoped someone else would champion Pete's cause. There was an extremely long pause. So long Walter started to open his mouth but alas he was saved by the sweet tone of Lillian Grainger.

"Ryan. You know I like to stay as active as I can. I realize, dear boy, that you have our best interest at heart. But Pete's right. This was a bit too strenuous.

"We had a good time, no doubting that, but right now, I feel like if I walk another step, I'll collapse and float away under the water. How about you revamp this game? Keep it friendly competition that will be good exercise, but maybe not so far? How about halfway up and then back. I think that might be better for everyone. Do you all agree?"

The men shook their heads, but no one spoke. It was as if Lillian were the beautiful starlet of the nineteen-forties and they were the stagehands. Just there to support her and do a good job.

"I apologize, everyone. I had no idea how you were feeling. I wanted to do something fun that would be healthy for you. It's funny because when I watch all of you, you amaze me. None of you are nearly what my vision of seventies, eighties, and even ninety would be. I pushed too hard. Please don't let this stop you from coming."

"Who said we were going to stop coming?" Lillian questioned.

"Yeah. She's right. No one said any such thing. We just need you to slow down a little. We understand this was your first time to the rodeo. You did a great job, kid. Maybe just a little too great." Polish Pete laughed.

Everyone agreed they would definitely still be there at nine a.m. sharp. Only no more Olympics. Ryan agreed and promised to keep things at an agreeable pace.

Walter was disappointed that he didn't get to talk with Lillian, but he was equally as happy that Norman didn't take the road to permanent residency. They packed up and headed home. They were all done for the day. Later that evening, Walter was enjoying some time alone on the porch. Given his current situation with Robert and Vivienne, the porch was actually warmer than the temperature inside. Ryan had pulled up next door and parked in his driveway. Walter said a quick but fleeting prayer that the kid would go inside, but he didn't. Instead, he cut across both lawns and landed on the steps to Walter's porch.

"Hi. How's your night?" Ryan sat down with his back to Walter.

"It's good, kid. How about you?"

"Not so much. It's really bothering me about earlier. I was reckless. I could have seriously hurt someone or worse. Honestly, I thought I was doing a good thing." He turned to face Walter.

"I know you did. And so does everyone else. You gotta stop beating yourself up. Everything is fine. Everyone is home and happy tonight. You learned something today. When we try to give you advice, it's not because we like the sound of our voices. It's because we've been where you're at right now," Walter stood up. "But what happened today was something no one anticipated. Not even you, Mr. Lifeguard. Move on, kid."

"I know. I get it. I can go over the top. Even Grace pulls in the reigns sometimes."

"You're a good kid, Ryan. You mean well. You'll figure it out." Walter shivered.

"Thanks. You going in?"

"Yeah. I think it's time."

"Me too. Goodnight. See you tomorrow?" Ryan waited.

"See you tomorrow, kid." Walter gave a quick wave. As he entered the subzero domain that had become home, he decided to go straight up to his room and sulk behind a closed door. At least he would enjoy the company.

Chapter Fourteen

The next several weeks flew by without any further ruckus. Lillian was looking a little better. Her color returned to a soft pink hue, and her energy was up. Vincent picked Walter up every morning, Monday through Friday, and they developed a nice routine of stopping for breakfast before hitting the pool.

Home life was the same. Walter didn't converse with them unless he absolutely had to, and Vivienne and Robert stayed clear of any space they didn't have to share with him. The place that once was home felt more like the lobby of a hotel. Strangers come and go, and you're only there for a few minutes to check in and out. He even went so far as to purchase a thirty-two-inch flat screen for his bedroom. Walmart had a sale on an Emerson for one hundred seventy-five dollars—a steal. Vincent helped him set it up, and his bedroom became his new go-to for all his shows.

Any new snowfall began to dissipate, becoming a memory stored away for the next year, and the sun shone a bit brighter and stayed around a little longer. Spring was on its way.

Walter enjoyed his time with Lillian immensely and started thinking maybe he would ask if she'd like to join him for dinner. As friends, of course. He wouldn't want to give her the wrong impression. That morning he decided to dab a small amount of cologne on his neck before dressing. When he got downstairs, Vivienne was sitting on the couch with her head in her hands.

He walked by her without saying a word and went to the kitchen for a glass of juice. Peeking around the edge of the doorway, he checked to see if she might be crying.

He couldn't tell. *Damn it*. He poured the orange thirst quencher into a small glass and gulped it down. Then washing the glass, he set it down on the rack to dry. He hesitated a few moments, trying to think of a way to break the silence without sounding too eager. He had nothing. Maybe I should just leave and not say anything, he thought, but what if something was seriously wrong? He wasn't sure if Vivienne would share with him freely.

Pursing his lips and taking in a deep breath, he walked into the center of the living room. She was in the same position.

"Are you alright?" Walter spoke in a soft tone.

He waited a few moments for an answer, but she didn't say a word.

"Vivienne. Is something wrong? Are you alright?" Vivienne lifted her head and turned to look at him.

Her face was stained with dried tears, and her eyes were puffy and red. That's when Walter noticed the little brown box on the floor by her right foot. John Adams Elementary School was in bold letters across the top. Walter stared at the box and then shifted his gaze to Vivienne. Her body was hunched over and so tightly withdrawn that she almost looked like a child. She reached down and grabbed the box, placing it in her lap. She hadn't opened it yet.

"Where did you get that?" Walter asked.

Vivienne caressed the box, and her body started to shake. Walter quickly sat down beside her, holding her tight. He tried to soothe with words he knew were empty, but he couldn't stop them from coming. When her body calmed to a whimper, she handed the box to Walter.

"Open it, please." Her hand was shaking.

Walter took the package and set it on the side table. Pulling a small pen knife from his pocket, he slit the box down the center.

Pulling the flap open on each side, he reached in and pulled out a small frame decorated with different shapes of pasta. It was painted in gold and in the center was a picture of Chase with his teacher. He had received an honor reward for being a good citizen in class. Vivienne took the frame from Walter's hands and clutched it to heart. Her body shook as the tears flowed down her cheek and gathered in little pools of wetness on her pants, leaving a polka dot pattern in the fabric.

Walter tilted his gaze toward the ceiling and quietly asked himself, *Why? How could you be so cruel? Damn you all to hell! He was a baby!* Swallowing to push back the emotions that were taking hold, he drew Vivienne in closer to his heart. He knew it would pass. Her body would give way to exhaustion soon.

When her body went limp, he took hold of her arm and stood up. Still clutching the frame, Vivienne let Walter lead her upstairs to her bedroom. Walter helped her into bed and drew the covers up. He leaned over and kissed her forehead before sliding the macaroni frame from her hands and placing it on the nightstand.

On the way down the stairs, Walter was startled by the doorbell. He figured it was probably Vincent. When he was at the landing, he walked over and peered out of the side window. Vincent was standing on the porch with his back to the door. Walter quickly unlocked it and motioned for his friend to come in.

"I hate to do this to you, but I'm going to have to cancel today. I don't want to leave Viv alone. We've had an incident."

"Oh no. Is she alright?" Vincent's voice cracked.

Walter explained to his friend the package delivery and its contents. Vincent just shook his head in agreement. There was really nothing that could be said.

"I'm sorry I couldn't call before you got here."

"No. Don't worry about it. Just take care of her. I'll pick you up tomorrow?"

"Yes. But if anything changes, I'll call you later."

"Please make my apologies to Lillian."

"You got it, my friend." The two men shook hands, and Walter closed the door.

He went into the kitchen and fixed some breakfast before setting up in front of the fantasy box in the living room. He had hoped some of his shows could take his mind far enough away to get through the morning.

It worked. By the time he realized the hour, it was one o'clock, and Vivienne ambled down the stairs.

She had a heavy winter sweater of Robert's wrapped around her body, losing her tiny frame in the bulky material. She smiled at Walter and took a seat on the couch. Curling her legs underneath, she sunk into the couch and reached for a magazine on the coffee table. Flipping through the pages, her eyes widened, and she chuckled softly.

Walter was at a loss for words. She clearly was a bit better, and he was horrified at the thought of saying the wrong thing and dredging up the emotions she had felt a few hours ago.

He hadn't noticed until the sleeve of her sweater fell back that she resumed clutching the frame.

Vivienne glanced over, and they locked eyes. Her head bent down toward the frame, and then back up to Walter.

"Dad. Could you do something for me?" She wiggled in the sweater.

"Of course."

"Would you please put this picture of Chase on the shelf with the others?" Vivienne gently ran her fingers over the ornaments, and then extended her hand.

Walter willingly took the frame and walked over to the bookcase. He found a spot next to a picture of Robert when he was ten. He carefully set it down and turned it slightly to the left. Then he turned and looked to Vivienne for approval. The corners of her mouth and eyes turned up as she tilted her head and admired it.

"It's perfect. Thank you."

Walter tried to rub the tightness out of his chest, but it lingered. He struggled to swallow past the lump in his throat.

"Vivienne. I'm sorry. I ..."

She put her hand up to stop his words.

"It's okay. We're gonna be fine." She averted her eyes back to the magazine, "How does roasted chicken with those little potatoes you like sound for dinner?"

"Delicious. But how about we go out tonight? Don't cook. My treat." Walter's heart felt lighter. He had missed their chats.

"You know what? I think tonight I'm going to take you up on that. Robert's working late, so it'll just be you and me. Is that alright?"

"Well, what do you know? I get the company of a beautiful woman all to myself. Sounds great."

Vivienne laughed, softening the melody of the room and Walter's anxiety.

"How about I pick you up at six o'clock, Madam?" Walter bowed.

"Six would be lovely, kind sir. Shall I dress formally, or is this a relaxed venue we will be dining?"

"Does the lady have a preference?" Walter sat down in his chair.

"The lady does. She says... Burger Bills."

"Madam, you have impeccable taste."

Vivienne stood up, and still laughing, she curtsied. The phone rang, and she ran off to the kitchen to answer it. Walter felt lighter than he had in days. He knew the dark cloud would follow her and Robert for as long as they walked the planet, but maybe there could be more light in the coming years. The effects of their last conflict had melted away today because of a common bond. One beautiful little boy. Maybe he could walk them all into the sunshine. Walter prayed for redemption and forgiveness, but most of all—peace.

Vivienne came in and sat down. The look of contemplation gave him pause.

"Oh no. Please don't tell me it's bad news."

"Not exactly." Vivienne knitted her brows, gazing into blank space.

"You appear to have something to say. What is it?" Walter waited.

"Well—I need to speak with Robert first. But I will tell you later tonight. Are we still on for dinner?"

"Sure. I'm tasting those burgers now." Walter licked his lips.

"Great. I have some errands to run. I'll be back around five. Do you need anything?"

Things are back to normal, thought Walter. "No. I'm good. Be careful; it's dreary out there."

"I will. I'm gonna go and throw some clothes on. I'll be down in a minute." Vivienne ran up the stairs.

Walter sat back. *What was so cryptic about the phone call that she had to wait? Huh. No use getting worked up. She seems fine.* He pushed the thoughts from his head and turned his attention to the TV and the latest repeat of *Criminal Minds*.

A few minutes later, Vivienne came charging down the stairs and threw on a hat and coat before kissing Walter on the cheek and slamming the door shut.

Two episodes into *Criminal Minds*, his eyes closed with a blanket of sleep resting on them, and his body floated weightlessly, surrounded by darkness and the sound of —screams.

Walter heard his name in the distance. Turning, the darkness clouded his vision. He squinted his eyes; the voice grew louder.

"Dad. Dad. Wake up. You okay?"

He fluttered his eyes until they opened, the small frame of his daughter-in-law was standing over him.

"You were moaning. Are you in pain?" Vivienne's forehead wrinkled.

"No. No. I'm fine. I was dreaming about the ocean. Remember when Gina and I went to Atlantic City with Frank and Elsa? Gina had slipped and was pulled out with the tide. I was yelling to her."

"Oh. You had me worried. Did you save Mom?" Vivienne sat beside him on the carpet.

"I wish I could say I was the gallant hero in this story, but Frank got to her before me. He was a champion swimmer. Won a bunch of medals." Walter grinned.

"Okay. I'm going to go upstairs and freshen up. It's about ten minutes past five. We still going at six?"

"Yep. I will be waiting at the front door at six sharp."

Vivienne rolled her eyes and snickered. When she was out of the room, Walter breathed in and held it for a moment before exhaling. He had lied to his daughter-in-law. His dream was not of the ocean or Gina. It was about that day. But he couldn't tell her. Especially not after this morning. He tilted his head back and rested it on the billowy chair cushion. Closing his eyes, he played back that day with precision recall.

Every move and counter move reconstructed to an inevitable end. He shivered, and then stood up to shake off the feelings. They had begun to grip him, and he didn't want to ruin Vivienne's night out.

Hell would have to wait until he slept tonight.

It had been a long time since he had spent such a lovely evening with his daughter-in-law. Their dinner of burgers, fries, and apple pie for dessert was a greasy, sweet slice of paradise. Afterward, they decided it had been too long since seeing a movie, so off to the theater they went. Two hours of swashbuckling adventure, and they were both ready for the comfort of their own beds and rumpled pillows.

As they approached the front door, Robert's snores were so loud they could be heard from the porch. They both burst into laughter as Vivienne turned the key and then slammed the door, startling Robert intentionally.

"Hi, sleepy head." Vivienne bent down and kissed him on the lips.

"Hey, you guys are back. Did you have fun? How was the movie?" Robert yawned.

"The movie was great. Come on, get up. You and I have a date with our cozy bed. I'm exhausted. Goodnight, Dad." They both waved as they went upstairs.

Walter went into the kitchen and got his usual bedside glass of water. He then dimmed the living room light and followed their trail.

His bed was warm, and he flipped the covers up and over his body until they nestled under his chin. He shuddered a little when he thought of what awaited him. Maybe this time, he could make a different outcome ... only in his dreams.

The nightmare ended as it always did, with death being its permanent finale. Walter stirred, struggling to break free of the constraints that had wrapped him in a cocoon of cotton.

The morning sun crept through the room, draping golden goodness over everything it touched. His forehead beaded up with sweat. He wiped away the moisture as he struggled to open his eyes. The sleep hangover was deep and held on tight this morning. When he was able, he stretched and swung his legs down onto the wood floor. Today it felt warm. A nice change from the cold he had endured the past few months. Reaching for his cane, he steadied his legs and pushed his body to an upright position. His legs and arms moving like they were encased in cement meant it was going to be a rough day. Hopefully, the water in the pool wasn't chilly, and he could work out the stiffness.

A whiff of the many layers of spices and herbs streaming through the house tickled his taste buds as he opened the bedroom door. Vivienne was feeling better. Breakfast as usual was a ritual Walter welcomed. He enjoyed his morning stop at the diner with Vincent, but nothing beat Viv's cooking. He grabbed his phone and called Vincent. After explaining the reason why he would be missing their new routine, Vincent completely understood. He agreed to pick him up at eight-thirty instead of the usual seven-forty-five.

Walter took a lukewarm shower for the first time since September said its goodbyes. In steady pulsing streams, the water hit the top of his head and trickled down his back, doing little for his joints, but, nonetheless, soothing his soul. Spring would be here soon, and with it, the birth of things to come. Walter was tired of the dreary, cold days and long bitter nights. He longed for the change. When he was dressing, he chose a light blue, button-up short sleeve shirt. Maybe he was in denial. After all, the new appearance of sunlight in the morning wasn't exactly the announcement that spring had arrived, but he didn't care. Besides, he'd have his coat on.

Walter whistled his Gina's favorite song as he descended the stairs and into the caressing scent of bacon and eggs. Entering the kitchen, Vivienne greeted him with a bright smile and a cup of coffee. He took a seat at the table next to Robert, who had lingered, choosing breakfast over beating the early morning traffic.

She set down a plate containing four strips of bacon, scrambled eggs with cheese melted over the top, and two slices of rye toast. Walter closed his eyes and took in the layers of scent before digging into the superb goo of melted cheese and eggs.

"Late today, Son?" Walter took a sip of coffee.

"Actually, I've decided to stay home today. Called in sick. Viv and I are going to drive up to the village for the day."

Walter was stunned. Robert never missed work. He literally had to be too ill to walk to call in sick. The only time Walter could remember Robert missing work due to illness was when he had appendicitis. And that took some convincing on Vivienne's part to get him to the hospital. His work ethic was commendable but sometimes borderline absurd.

"You are missing work to go play? What's wrong?" Walter set down his fork.

"Nothing. Honestly, everything is good."

"I'm not buying it. You two are up to something. Spill," Walter insisted.

Vivienne put down her plate and poured coffee into a mug before taking a seat next to Robert. She reached out and took his hand. He clasped hers and squeezed.

Walter observed this and braced for the worse. He knew Viv had been to the doctor and undergone several tests. His heart raced in his chest, and his hands trembled with the thought he was about to be given some very bad news. Robert swallowed and took a swig of orange juice. A drink of choice when he ate eggs.

"Dad. I know things have been strained lately, and we've all been through the wringer and back. You know Vivienne hasn't been feeling well lately."

Oh, God. Here it comes, thought Walter

"We were going to wait another month before telling you, but since you've insisted and judging by your tone, you think it's bad. It's not. Vivienne's pregnant." Robert reached over and hugged his wife.

Walter could feel the sting on his cheek from the verbal slap in the face. He had no words.

"Say something. Isn't this great news?" Robert's eyes widened.

"I uh ... I need to get ready. Vincent will be here shortly. Enjoy your day."

Walter got up and didn't look back at either of them. His heart ached from the stabbing pain that bewildered him. *I should be elated. A new life in the family.* But he couldn't feel anything but all-consuming anger. Vincent's timing couldn't have been better. As soon as Walter put on his coat, he heard the beeping of the car horn. He peeled back the curtain to see the car's fumes floating through the air in a puff of white smoke.

"Dad. Stop." Robert was in the living room.

"Vincent is waiting. I've got to go." Walter reached for the doorknob.

"He can wait a second. What was that in the kitchen? We thought you'd be happy. What's going on with you?" Robert raised a brow.

"I don't know. I don't want to talk about it right now." Walter opened the door. "I'll see you later."

Before Robert could respond, Walter left.

He'd left his son in a state of confusion. But he felt no words were better than angry ones. He'd talk to both of them later; first, he needed to figure out why he felt this way.

When they got to the center, the parking lot had five cars. He recognized all of them. They belonged to the senior crowd. Walter was relieved. He wasn't in the mood for toddlers and teens. A quick change, and he was at the first step of the pool's low end.

What used to take him a good twenty minutes now only took ten. He had his routine down to a science.

Lillian was sitting on a lounge by herself. He gestured for her to join him. She held up five fingers— she'd be there in five minutes. He chatted with Vincent and Norman, who was floating on a Boogie board.

"Doc told me to use this board and kick. He says it will help with the circulation in my legs. They feel like lead weights in the morning." Norman splashed lightly with his feet.

"And is it helping?" Vincent inquired.

"Not sure. This is only my second day. I guess maybe a little. I slept better last night." Norman stood up and bounced up and down.

"That's because you were probably dog-tired from all the kicking."

The other two shook their heads and laughed.

"You boys seem to be having a good time. What's so funny?" Lillian sat down on the middle step.

Walter swam over and then sat down on the step below her.

"We were discussing Norm's new activity. Doc has him paddling with the board. He said he slept better last night. We think it was because he was exhausted. Not sure if it's helping his legs, though."

"Well, never you mind what these two say, Norman. You keep it up. If you sleep better, you feel better. It must be helping." Lillian slid into the water.

"Thank you, Lillian," Norman splashed water at Vincent and Walter. "The lady knows what she's talking about."

"We're not going to argue with that," Walter and Vincent were in unison.

Walter tried to be light and enjoy the company of his friends, but Robert and Vivienne's news loomed in the back of his head, overshadowing and distracting him. Lillian must have sensed something was up because she cornered him with the question.

"What has got you so far away?" Lillian treaded water beside him.

"What do you mean? I'm just enjoying the peace. It's quiet today without all the ruckus of the teeny ones." Walter turned away. He hated lying to her.

"I've known you a long time, friend. That means I know when you're handing out a bunch of bull. Now, if you don't want to discuss it, then fine. Say so. But don't lie to me. That's just an insult to my intelligence." Lillian pursed her lips.

"Have you ever heard news that should excite you or make you feel happy, and the opposite happens?" Walter coughed.

"I'm not entirely sure what you're talking about, but it seems something upset you this morning. However, what you perceive you should feel has very little to do with what you do feel. Do you know why this incident is affecting you the way it is?"

Lillian held on to the edge of the pool and gently kicked her legs under the water.

"That's the problem. I haven't a clue. It's surprising me, actually. This morning, Robert and Vivienne announced they are having a baby. They were elated. All I felt was anger. I don't think I should be saying anything because they had wanted to wait another month into the pregnancy before making an announcement. But it's eating me up. Please keep this to yourself," Walter sighed.

"Of course." Lillian reached out and held Walter's hand. She wound her fingers through his, and then with the other hand, gently cupped his cheek. "My dear friend. You've had a tragedy that no words can soothe. And so have they. Greater perhaps. Do you think they are trying to replace Chase?"

"No. I don't. Well, maybe. I don't know. I feel so damn angry most of the time." Walter put his head down. "Then there's the guilt. Why?"

"Why what?' Lillian said gently.

"Why, God damn it, am I here? I'm an old man. He was a little boy. A baby. Our baby. How can they live with me knowing I survived and their baby didn't? I failed them," Walter's voice cracked as tears trickled down his cheek.

"Walter, you're not angry with them for the pregnancy. You're angry with yourself." Lillian's eyes teared up.

"Hey, you two okay over here?" Norman swam up to them.

"Yes. Please give us a minute, Norman," Lillian said politely.

Norman nodded and swam away.

"Walter. What happened was not your fault. It was *his* fault. The one who brought this pain to all of you. Chase knows his papa did everything he could. He loved you so much. You will see him again. But for now, it's your job to welcome his baby sister or brother into this world and be the same kind of grandpa you were to him. Tell them all about their big brother. How smart and funny he was. How you two were best friends. That is what you need to do," Lillian's words stumbled through her tears.

Walter enfolded her in his arms, and she held on tight. Then pulling back, without any awkwardness, he gently kissed her on the lips. Lillian pulled back and then slowly moved in and kissed him back.

The couple floated at the pool's edge in silence for quite a while. Walter wasn't sure what had just happened or what it meant, but he knew his anger had melted, carried away by the fluttering of his heart.

Walter enjoyed the rest of the day at the pool with Lillian. They never spoke of their chance kiss, but neither one left the other's side all day.

Norman and Vincent had stayed clear for a while, but Walter knew their curiosity would get the best of them. Within half an hour, they joined the pair. They were both good guys, and Walter wanted to tell them the news, but he knew he needed to wait for Robert's okay. He had already pushed it by telling Lillian.

At the end of the day, Walter got up enough gumption to ask Lillian to dinner. She accepted, and they set plans for Friday evening. Since he no longer drove, Lillian insisted she pick him up. Walter felt a little funny. He wasn't accustomed to this role reversal. But after much persuasion from Lillian as to the stupidity of his male ego, he agreed.

On the ride home, Vincent didn't ask any questions about their encounter or Walter's earlier mood. He was the best kind of friend. Always loyal and never pushy. Walter thought back to the day they first met. He and Gina had been living in the neighborhood for about two weeks, and their car broke down. Walter took it to the local garage, and Vincent was the owner. They struck up a friendship immediately. Two ex-marines and Korean War vets. Vincent's wife, Marie, had been a sweet girl. She was almost ten years younger than him, and she looked up to Gina like an older sister. The couples, along with Frank and Elsa, were inseparable. They had so much fun back then.

Every Friday night was date night, and the guys would take their wives to dinner and a movie. Sometimes, they ditched the movie for dancing. Then on Saturday night, it was a game of Bridge. A common card game they'd play until the wee hours of the morning, alternating houses.

When Marie passed away fifteen years ago, Vincent threw himself into his business. It worked for about the first ten years, and then it became too much. With his age slowing him down, he sold the garage. Neither son wanted to take it over, and his daughter lived in Connecticut with her husband, the plumber, and their two kids. He never dated or mentioned another woman. Vincent was completely devoted to Marie and her memory.

When Walter arrived home, Robert's SUV was gone. He knew that meant they were still in the village. The porch light was left on, and when he stepped into the entry, the light for the living room was dimly lit.

Walter walked over to the dial on the wall and turned up the volume of light before going upstairs to shower and put on some comfy flannels. Although the sun had warmed the day, it was still early enough in the year to have the cold push its way through at night.

When he was done, he went into the kitchen to fix something to eat. There was a note from Vivienne under a magnet on the refrigerator. She had made a plate of leftovers from breakfast. All he had to do was pop it in the microwave and fix some toast. Walter's stomach growled as he buttered and jellied his two slices of rye. Then placing them on the plate, he went into the living room and set himself up in front of the TV. He was on his last bite when he heard the key and the deadbolt unlock. Robert and Vivienne came in with smiles.

Walter set down his fork and wiped his mouth with a napkin.

"Thank you for making my plate, Vivienne." He smiled nervously.

"You're welcome. Was it alright heating in the microwave?"

"Yes, it was delicious. Can I talk to the two of you for a minute?" Walter cleared his throat.

"Sure." They both sat down on the couch.

"First. How was your day? Did you have a nice time?" Walter was stalling.

They both shook their heads yes. "What's up?" Robert asked.

"I need to apologize for earlier. I'm sorry. I was just taken off guard. I didn't mean to seem like I wasn't happy. This is wonderful news. It's just…"

"Don't worry. We understand." Robert patted Walter's knee.

"We were surprised too. Vivienne didn't know how to handle it when the doctor told her. We both wrestled with the idea. We're not young kids. There are certain health risks for her with a pregnancy in her forties. But this is a gift that we both want. And in no way is this an attempt to replace our boy. No one can do that," Robert stumbled over the last sentence, and Vivienne put her arm around him.

"When is the happy month?" Walter swiped a tear from the corner of his eye.

"The end of October. We're having a Halloween baby," Vivienne screeched.

"Wonderful!" Walter grinned ear to ear.

"Yup. It's going to be a long summer," Vivienne laughed.

"We'll find ways to keep you cool," Robert chimed in.

"I think it's time we get some air conditioning in this old house," Walter suggested.

"Actually, that's a good idea," Robert agreed.

"Whoa, you two. That's going to be much too expensive. I'll be fine. We have the window unit in the bedroom and this one in the living room. That's good enough. We have a baby to plan for, and we need everything."

Both men reluctantly agreed.

Walter sat back, his eyes scanning the pictures on the shelf. *The house was about to get turned upside down. In a good way. In the best possible way.*

Chapter Fifteen

Friday night came quickly, and before Walter knew it, Lillian was beeping her car's horn in the driveway. He said goodnight to Robert and Vivienne and barely escaped with a few teasing words from Robert on his way out the front door.

Lillian looked absolutely beautiful. She wore a black velvet coat and a little cloche hat decorated with a small burgundy flower and gray feather to the side. Walter admired the hat. He wondered why women didn't dress like this anymore. It was so elegant and polished. When he was securely belted, Lillian backed out of the driveway.

"Sir. Would you please tell me where we are going?" Lillian said coyly.

"Nope. But I'll direct you." Walter wiggled his shoulders, trying to calm the sting in his cheeks.

"I'm intrigued. I hope I'm dressed appropriately."

"You look lovely. Perfect for the evening."

They drove for about thirty minutes with Walter as the perfect backseat driver. Lillian paid close attention to the road and his directions. Night driving was more difficult on her aging eyes. As she pulled into a long driveway, it appeared deserted. Walter pointed to a winding road, and Lillian followed the path. At its end was a large brick mansion with colonial columns and a horse and buggy out front.

"We have arrived, madam."

"Walter. This is Chestwood Manor. It's impossible to get reservations. You have to book almost a year in advance. How did you manage this?"

"The owner is an old marine buddy. We served in Korea together." Walter's chest noticeably swelled.

A gentleman came up to the car, opened Lillian's door, and took her keys. He asked for her last name and wrote it on a small card that he then tore in half. Her portion had a number on it.

Lillian placed it in her purse and then clutched the arm Walter so gallantly offered.

"If you'd like, we can go for a carriage ride after dinner." Walter pointed to the waiting buggy.

"Oh, how lovely," Lillian gushed.

They took their time approaching the large white doors held open by a gentleman dressed in a black suit. It was like a vision out of a fairy tale begging to be savored. The strings of soft lights in the trees and the crunch of gravel under their heels both looked and sounded extravagant. As they stepped up to the jewel-tone greens and burgundies of the interior foyer, they were escorted by yet another well-dressed man to the reservation desk. Walter gave his last name, and in moments, they were being ushered to their table.

Their booth was perfect for two and placed next to a floor-to-ceiling cathedral window. Walter first assisted Lillian with her coat and hung it on a thick bronze hook at the end of their booth. He removed his coat, revealing a dark gray suit with a pale blue shirt and gray and blue patterned tie. After hanging his jacket, he slid into the seat. Lillian was gazing out the window. The garden surrounding the manor was magnificent by night. She could not take her eyes off the velvety flowers and ropes of vines that displayed their dusky hues by soft solar lights expertly hidden deep in the foliage. At intervals amongst the winding paths, weathered stone benches invited lovers into an old-world charm and a place to steal away a soft kiss.

"It's magical. As if fairies are nestled safely in their homes hidden in the trees, asleep until morning." Lillian's voice was barely above a whisper.

"It is special, isn't it?"

Walter was brought back to Disneyland, and the night he spent with Chase. It was magical.

"Walter." A burly short man came to the table with his arms extended.

"Ralphie!" Walter got up and hugged the jovial man.

"This must be the lovely, Lillian." Ralphie bent over and kissed her hand.

"Still the operator, I see," Walter ribbed him.

"Stop. I know a beauty when I see one. Did this guy tell you he saved my life in the war?"

"No. He sure didn't." Her eyes traveled from Ralphie to Walter.

"We were dug in, and our trench was bombarded with artillery from the other side. We were like sitting ducks. Our Lieutenant ordered us to pull back until reinforcement came. I made one move, and I was hit. I'll spare you the gory details, but if it weren't for this guy, I wouldn't be standing here today." Ralphie hugged Walter again.

"Enough. It was a flesh wound." Walter sat down.

"The hell it was. Miss Lillian, you order whatever you want. And you have to get dessert. I have the best for fifty miles around. As always my friend, it's my pleasure. Enjoy your evening. And take the lady for a carriage ride after dinner, you old son of a bitch. Oh, excuse my language, Lillian." Ralphie bowed.

"It's perfectly fine. Thank you so much for sharing your beautiful restaurant with us." Lillian smiled warmly.

Ralphie left, and Walter fidgeted with his napkin. He knew the question that was coming next.

"Walter. How come you never told me you saved a man's life?" Lillian glanced at the menu.

"The war is something I don't like talking about. Things happened there that are better left staying there. It was something I wish no one would ever have to do again."

Walter switched subjects, "So, does anything look appetizing?" He opened the menu.

"I should say. How about everything," Lillian chuckled.

Lillian decided on the mushroom ravioli in a cream sauce with the house salad and a glass of white wine. Being the meat lover, Walter chose a half-pound New York cut with baked potato, green beans, and a glass of Merlot. He didn't drink wine often, but loved a good red when it was paired with a thick, juicy steak. Instead of salad, he ordered the soup. The chef's special, beef barley, was the perfect starter.

The waiter, Timothy, brought two small loaves of bread and butter. The bread was still hot, and the butter melted into each crevice. Any leftover liquid goodness drizzled down the sides.

Walter served Lillian a slice before buttering some for himself. The wine was smooth and the conversation smoother. Walter was having the best night in years. Lillian was such a refined lady and so interesting to talk to. He allowed a memory of Gina to drift into his mind for just a moment. He felt perfectly comfortable with Lillian, and it provoked a twinge of guilt. He let it go. He had to.

Dinner was not only delicious but filled their appetite to capacity. The meal could have ended right there, but Ralphie insisted on dessert. He sent the cart over for Lillian to choose. Walter gave her the reigns. Lillian selected Crème Brule and requested two dessert spoons.

Walter was a chocolate man himself, but he was pleasantly surprised by how good the crunchy caramelized sugar top tasted with the creamy warm center. This one varied slightly from the version Lillian had eaten in the past. Chunks of pineapple and maraschino cherries at the bottom of the bowl tantalized her taste buds and were a welcome delight. She professed it was the best Crème Brule she had ever eaten. Ralphie was thrilled.

Walter paid the check, and led Lillian to the waiting horse and carriage. Lillian took a step up as she held onto Walter's arm; the footboard was worn but sturdy enough for the both of them. Once inside, they sat on a soft blue and gold tapestry-covered bench and reached for a large flannel blanket. It was just the right size for snuggling. The carriage slightly swayed as the ride began. The only noise to be heard was the clomp of horse hooves and the occasional click of the driver as he directed the silver stallion through the narrow pathways. Lillian reached out and allowed wispy ferns to tickle her hands. As she tilted her head back, she saw the traveling canopy of maple and oak branches above them. Walter was enthralled by the variety of flowers following their journey. He couldn't decide if purple or white were the best to present to Lillian. In the end, the soft pink tea rose caught his eye, and he plucked a single bloom to give to her. He placed it in her upturned hand. She turned her head towards him as her lips curved in a gentle smile.

She scooted even closer to Walter and looked into his eyes. In her gaze, he saw a familiar reflection ... family. He bent down and kissed her lips softly and then her forehead. She laid her head on his shoulder and basked in the perfect silence of magic.

When the ride was over, he held her arm as she stepped down from the carriage, and they took their time walking hand in hand to the valet. When the car came, Walter opened the door for Lillian, tipped the valet boy, and tucked himself in the passenger seat.

He wasn't ready for the evening to end, but there were gray shadows of fatigue under Lillian's eyes that were not there earlier in the evening. She was tired.

The following day was Lillian's chemotherapy treatment. More doses of killing her to save her. Nausea would steal her vitality and hold it captive for days. The pool was on hold, much like the rest of her life. Walter offered to come over and keep her company, and she accepted. He also volunteered to take her to the treatment, well, he volunteered Vivienne to drive them, but her niece was already at the house. She drove in from the Island and stayed overnight so she would be there for the early morning appointment.

Walter's heart sank. He wanted to help. But she assured him that coming over during the recoup time after chemo would help her tremendously. He reached out and touched the top of her hand. She held it for a moment, and then placed it back on the steering wheel.

When they reached his house, he hesitated before getting out. Here it was... the end of the evening and he wasn't ready. He asked her to please call him when she arrived home so he knew she was safe. She nodded yes. He angled his face toward her mouth and placed his lips on hers. They lingered, allowing the warmth to reach their hearts.

She softly touched his face, gently gliding her hand across his cheek and jawline. Walter tingled. He felt renewed. His senses were awoken from a long slumber. Closing the car door after stealing one last kiss, he practically skipped up the steps on his way into the house. Life was good, damn good.

He waited impatiently for the next fifteen minutes until he got the confirmation call that she was home and safely inside. He whispered sweet dreams and placed the receiver down. He brushed the phone with his hand, almost as if Lillian could feel it. As he turned away from his reverie, he saw Robert standing behind him.

"Don't say a word," Walter muttered.

"Say what? I wasn't gonna say anything," Robert teased. "Hey Viv, come down here. I think Dad's got a girlfriend."

"What?" Vivienne yelled from upstairs.

"Stop it. Nothing Vivienne. Go to sleep. Your husband is being an ass." Walter squirmed. "Go to bed, Robert."

Walter started up the stairs.

"Sure. Whatever you say. But does this mean if things work out, I'll have to call her Mom? Because you know I don't think…"

"Robert!" Walter yelled.

Robert eased off and went into the kitchen. Walter went to his bedroom. After he had brushed his teeth and put on his pajamas, he turned on the TV for background noise. Soon, he was drifting off with thoughts of Lillian, a new baby, and Sheldon Cooper's voice lulling him into a newfound happiness.

He woke feeling invigorated. No dark dreams to leave him with sweat-stained sheets. Sunshine and possibilities, she had lit a fire in his soul. He couldn't wait to get to the pool and spend another day with Lillian. Treatment was brutal, and Walter was happy when Lillian finally felt well enough to resume their waterside courtship. Over the next few weeks, their morning pool rendezvous spilled over into the evenings. Walter would usually find himself having dinner at Lillian's. Afterward, they'd watch a movie or sit on her back patio and talk for hours if it wasn't chilly.

It was Friday, March thirty-first. Easter was less than a month away, and Vivienne and Robert had invited the entire family over for dinner. Walter wrestled with the idea of asking Lillian. He had been so happy the past few weeks, yet a part of him felt guilty. He could never forget his Gina. She was the love of his life, but this woman, this powerhouse of grit and grace, had sparked a zest for life within him. A flame he believed to be extinguished.

They had finished dinner and decided the night was perfect for the patio. Lillian brought out a bottle of Cabernet, and Walter popped the cork. Pouring into the two wine glasses she had set on the glass coffee table, they toasted the evening and took a sip.

If I extend the invitation for an Easter celebration, would it feel strange bringing another woman to the house? Would the kids resent sharing a family holiday with a woman that wasn't their mother? I know Robert and Vivienne seem okay with it. Robert's relentless teasing is a giant clue. But what about the older boys? They may not be as understanding as their younger sibling.

The thoughts raced around in his head, making a muddy mess. Trying to subdue the confusion, he turned his attention to Lillian. He hadn't noticed at dinner, but she looked a little gaunt. Her petite frame highlighted the price of treatment. He cupped her hand in his. Bringing it up to his lips, he softly kissed it several times. Lillian's eyes smiled and twinkled in the moonlight.

"Are you feeling okay tonight?" Walter spoke in a tender voice.

Lillian paused and then looked to the stars.

"I told the doctor at treatment today that I've had enough. It's not working." Her smile didn't reach her eyes.

Walter squeezed her hand ever so lightly and then kissed it one more time. He said nothing. There would be a time for them to say goodbye, but not now. Lillian was saying it on *her* own terms. He needed to support her and enjoy every minute they had together.

"Robert and Vivienne are having Easter dinner at the house. I was wondering if you wouldn't mind accompanying me."

Walter stood up and stretched out his arm.

Lillian rose, and he pulled her close. They began to waltz to the music of the night air.

"I would love to," she whispered in his ear.

He bent down and, starting at the top of her cheekbone, caressed her face with his lips until they met hers. Walter's body shook with the tantalizing surge of life, carrying a jolt to his heart. He desired her. To feel her head nestled on his chest, the sweet taste of her salty skin. He pulled back and gazed into her eyes, searching for confirmation.

Lillian took his hand and led him into the house and to the moonlit shadows of her bedroom.

Easter Sunday was a tornado of preparation at the Reilly household. Vivienne had the ham in the oven at seven-thirty sharp. Robert made sure the newly mowed lawn had been raked to pave the way for the annual egg hunt.

Walter helped by setting out the paper dessert plates, napkins, and plastic forks. Vivienne used to despise the cheap stand-in for china, but lately, the cleanup was too much work. Paper was the only way to go.

Dinner was at three o'clock, and Walter went up to shower and change before the family arrived. Everyone usually showed up an hour early so the kids could open their Easter baskets and have the egg hunt. Robert had gone shopping for prizes at the Dollar Store. They were only small trinkets, but the kids loved them.

Walter's two older boys, Richard and Frank, arrived with their wives first. Their kids, all grown, were scattered across the map, but it was endearing watching the younger ones consume their Easter candy.

A few minutes later, Vivienne's brother, Jim, arrived with his wife, Samantha, and their two kids, Sadie, who was four, and Derek, seven. Vivienne had also invited two other close friends and their families. Altogether, five children aged eight to eleven were more than ready for added treats. Thankfully there were plenty of eggs to hide.

Walter had just finished dabbing his cologne when he heard the doorbell ring once again.

Looking in the mirror one last time, he brushed his hair to the side with his fingertips and smoothed his brows. He was ready.

When he was midway down the staircase, he spotted her. Lillian was standing in the entryway of the front door. Robert was helping her remove her sweater. Underneath, she wore a delicate pale green floral dress accented with ivory lace gloves. A tightly woven ivory hat adorned with a buttercup ribbon and a white gardenia complimented the ensemble. Walter's heart pitter-pattered the closer he got to her.

He bent down and gently kissed her cheek. Lillian's face blushed pink when she caught Robert winking at his dad.

Walter anxiously walked her through the house to the backyard, where the mob of family was hanging out.

"Everyone, I'd like you to meet my friend, Lillian," Walter slipped his hand in hers.

"Lillian Grainger. I remember you." Richard came over and hugged her.

"Me too. You gave out the best candy on Halloween," Frank laughed.

Walter's body relaxed, letting in the peace of a happy family gathering.

"Dad. Offer the lady a seat." Vivienne set a bowl of fruit on the table.

Flustered, Walter pulled out a chair at one of the round tables. Robert had rented banquet tables, folding chairs, and two long tables for food. The house wouldn't accommodate everyone, and he and Viv decided a lawn party would be a nice change after the confines of winter.

Luck was on their side, and it was a mild seventy-two degrees with plenty of sunshine.

He couldn't help but gaze at Lillian. The sky's golden rays cascaded over her shoulder, drenching her pure white locks in their glow. Her hair was always so shiny and silky, capturing the light as she turned her head. Lillian caught his eyes, and her cheeks glowed. She giggled lightly and turned her attention to the children's egg hunt.

"Lillian, we are so glad you decided to join us." Vivienne set down a bouquet of flowers.

"I am too. What lovely flowers."

Lillian reached out and softly glided her fingertips over the petals.

"Thank you. They're from Robert's brother Frank and his wife, Marcie. I think they're a perfect spring bouquet."

"Yes, they are. Is there something I can help you with, dear?"

"Nope. You just sit and enjoy the day. We have plenty of food coming out shortly. And thank you so much for the scrumptious pastries. You better watch Walter, though. They are his weakness."

Walter thought of a snarky comeback, but he wasn't in the mood for taunting. He felt too good, and Viv looked so happy. Her face was lit up from the love that surrounded her.

"I'll be just fine. I promise," Walter chuckled. "Would you like something to drink? I know Vivienne has tea and coffee brewing in the kitchen. Or a cold drink, maybe?" Walter waited for Lillian to answer.

"I would love a cup of tea if it's not too much trouble."

"None at all." Walter hastily went inside the house.

Minutes later, he came out with a silver tray containing a dainty cup and saucer filled with hot water. He had several tea bags beside the cup, a small floral creamer, and a crystal bowl with sugar cubes.

Also scattered about the tray were little pink and blue packets in case she preferred not to have sugar. Walter set the tray down in the center of the table in front of Lillian. He carefully removed the teacup and set the creamer and selected tea bags beside it. Then he put the bowl of sugar and alternative sweetener next to the creamer.

"The water is very hot, be careful." He shifted the cup a little closer to her.

"Thank you. This is lovely. Now let me see. Which tea will I have today? Ah. Earl Gray. I love a nice cup of Earl Gray. So soothing."

Walter watched attentively as Lillian steeped the packet of tea and then added cream and one sugar cube. *Hmm, she prefers the real stuff,* he thought.

"Walter, are you having anything?" Lillian smiled.

"I'm waiting on the coffee. It's almost done brewing."

"Not a tea man?"

"Not really. I prefer a stiff cup of Joe. Once in a blue moon, if I'm having the chills, I might grab a cup of tea. But that is very rare. How's your tea?"

"Wonderful. The children seem to be having a world of fun." Her eyes followed them as they searched for the hidden eggs.

"They do. This is a Reilly family tradition. Every Easter. I wonder who has more fun. The kids or Robert when he hides the eggs. Chase always peeks ... peeked. He would peek out of the back window to see if he could get a jump on all the hiding spots," Walter's voice cracked.

Lillian grasped his hand and held it tight.

Damn. I was having such a good day, Walter thought.

"Are you alright, Walter?" Her voice was soothing.

"I will be. Just takes a moment. Sometimes for that split second, I forget."

"He was such a good boy." Lillian's eyes watered.

"Yes. He was." Walter pushed back the lump in his throat.

"Hey, what are you two talking about? You look so serious. This is not a day for that. Now, who wants a slice of ham?" Vivienne had the carving knife in one hand and a large fork in the other.

Walter had been taken away to the dark place for but a moment. Vivienne's exquisite platters of food were enough to bring him back. The ham had a crisp layer of crust surrounding the juicy meat. Little cherries and slices of pineapple were held on top with toothpicks. The aroma made his mouth water. A large bowl of freshly made mashed potatoes, green bean casserole, apple sauce, salad, rolls with butter, and sweet potatoes with little marshmallows completed the feast.

Walter took the plate set in front of Lillian and served her a little of everything. His motto was if you don't like it, then don't eat it, but you should really try everything. Lillian gracefully received the plate and set her napkin on her lap before digging in.

Walter helped Vivienne serve the rest of the family before sitting down with his plate.

Robert had been busy rounding up the kids and making sure no eggs were left behind. It happened one unfortunate Easter a few years ago. They didn't realize it until a nauseating stench filled the backyard. Robert had searched for nearly an hour before he discovered the culprit. Since then, he was diligent about counting the eggs that were found.

The table was bustling with several different conversations all at once. The kids were at their own table, but the sound carried and nestled itself right in Walter's ears He quietly ate, choosing not to interact. It was hard to hear; the voices intertwined like string on a ball, the layers growing with each word that lingers in the air.

He didn't want to end up irritating everyone with the constant request to repeat what they had said. He felt like Lillian must have a similar sentiment because she was as quiet as a mouse.

When dinner was just about over, the noise settled into a calm murmur. Vivienne started clearing the plates to make room for the delectable desserts waiting on the kitchen counter.

Lillian got up to help, but Vivienne insisted she sit back down.

Walter stood up and asked if she would like to join him in the garden area. She happily accepted. An ornate copper bench for two was tucked away amongst the lavish green azaleas and colorful hydrangeas. Lillian followed Walter to the hidden splendor. They took a seat on the bench, and he held his hand out. She tenderly slipped hers into his.

"Your family has grown so much. I remember Gina bringing the boys with her to the beauty parlor. She'd make sure they stopped at the candy store first for treats and comics. They were always so well-behaved." Her eyes twinkled.

"They are all good boys. Not perfect. They've had their moments over the years, but we were very lucky. They turned out alright. Are you having a nice time?"

"Immensely. Boy, can Vivienne cook. She reminds me of Gina."

"She does. Learned most of her recipes from her. But I wouldn't ever tell her that."

"Why not."

"Got to keep her on her toes,." Walter smirked.

"Nonsense. The way she treats you. The girl is gold. You should tell her every day what a gift she is," Lillian snapped.

"Okay, okay. I will try to be more forthcoming with Vivienne." He rubbed the back of her hand.

Lillian smiled and tilted her head in agreement.

"Is she doing okay? I mean, not okay. Is she getting through any better?"

"You don't have to watch your words. I know what you mean. She has her days. Sometimes she seems happy and getting by, and then there are other times she won't leave the bedroom. I honestly don't know how the two of them *do* get out of bed. She's always doting on Robert and me, though."

"Perhaps it helps to redirect her pain. You know, if she spends all her energy on the both of you, then she has nothing left by the end of the day to focus on her loss." Lillian patted his thigh.

"Could be. God, I wish I could go back." Walter slammed his fist on the arm of the bench.

"Don't do that," Lillian pleaded.

"What?"

"Carry the guilt like a badge of honor. You know that's an impossible wish. You are not responsible. How many times does one person need to hear the truth before accepting it? You are the most stubborn man I've ever met. Guilt will eat you up inside and rob you from enjoying your life and the people around you. The ones that are here *now*. How long will you go blindly into each day, never recognizing how important you are to those who love you?"

Lillian's words pierced through Walter's heart like a steel blade exiting an excruciatingly painful open wound. He knew his guilt led him to do and say the most horrible things at times. But he never realized that someone like Lillian could call him out and leave him exposed. His anger was raw and a side he hoped to keep tucked away when he was with her.

"I've upset you. I'm sorry." Walter let go of her hand.

"You big idiot." She grabbed his hand again. "I just worry about you. I don't want you to push everyone away."

"I'm not pushing you away. Am I?"

"No. But Walter, I won't be here forever. And you're going to need your family. And they need you too. You yourself said it was difficult to understand how Vivienne and Robert function. Don't you think having you here makes it easier? That's when you're not making their lives a living hell."

"First of all, you are not going anywhere just yet. And I will promise you I will try to be the best me I can. Is this subject closed?"

"It is."

Walter leaned over and kissed her forehead. She nestled into him and laid her head on his shoulder. His breath slowed to a calm pace. She was good for him. He hoped he could be the same for her.

Chapter Sixteen

A month passed, and Vivienne and Robert felt confident enough about the pregnancy to tell everyone. And when they said everyone, they meant the world. Or at least that was Walter's perception. The house phone didn't stop ringing for two days. Family, friends, friends of friends, even the postman found out somehow. Walter swore Robert probably took out an ad in the local paper. The house felt different. Viv was starting to show ever so slightly, and the more her belly grew, the more joyful she became.

Walter tried each day to keep his promise to Lillian. It wasn't easy at times, but he learned to hold his tongue. They lived in the present. He enjoyed every moment he got to spend with her.

The senior program would end in a few weeks to make way for the summer schedule. Kids were out of school, and parents needed a safe environment for activities. What better place than with their local lifeguards learning how to swim, play games, and release all their youthful energy?

It saddened Walter to think of his daily routine coming to an end. Sure, they could still go to the pool, but it would be crowded and loud. Two combinations that most of his friends and he didn't enjoy. To compensate, Walter came up with the idea of a summer breakfast club. He actually got the idea from watching the nineteen eighty-five John Hughes film. Of course, minus the school setting, teachers, and delinquent youth. Or at least that's what Walter called them. Three times a week, they were all going to meet at the diner at nine a.m. sharp.

They enjoy staying in touch and spending time together. He knew that for some of his buddies, that would be the only socializing they had. Lillian thought it was a superb idea.

Walter sprung his creative summer schedule to the other seniors at the pool. All but one agreed it was a great idea. Adolfo. He wanted to keep swimming and didn't mind the crowds or the high energy of the kids. Walter understood. Adolfo was ,after all, Adolfo. He was a sweet man who did things his own way.

"Well, you got them all on board." Lillian swam up to him.

"I know. I think I'm kind of surprised." Walter beamed.

"Surprised? Why?"

"I didn't think they'd really want to continue hanging out. You know. It was just a winter thing."

"Nooooo. They all look forward to coming as much as we do. This is where you go to feel alive. If we stopped and didn't see each other, we'd be back to lonely days in front of the television. This is really a good thing that Ryan and Grace started."

"It is. Don't tell them." Walter winked.

"Oh, you." Lillian slapped his chest lightly.

"Speaking of good ideas, how about you and me go catch a movie tonight? We can go to Sal's for pizza first." Walter put his arms around her tiny waist. "Hey, you losing weight?"

"Never you mind. I think I would love that. Do you have a movie in mind?"

"I think that new action movie with that guy I like is playing. Are you good with a shoot 'em up?"

"That guy? You mean Dwayne Johnson? Of course." Lillian grinned. "You really love his movies."

"I do. And you should eat an extra slice of pizza tonight." He clutched her fragile body and hugged her gently.

"I told you. Never mind. A girl's gotta keep her figure."

Walter laughed, but inside, his concern had shot up to alarm. He helped her climb the stairs to exit the pool. Once they were out, he popped over and retrieved their towels from the lounge chair they had parked them on. Wrapping her up snugly, he escorted her to one of the chase lounges. He then took his towel and dried off as best he could. They sat relaxing until the bell sounded for the pool lanes to change for the swim team.

Every day at three o'clock, the local high school team came to practice. That was the time all the seniors gathered their belongings and got out as quickly as they could. The place became a teenage recipe for social upheaval.

Lillian shuffled to the women's locker room slower than usual. Walter could do nothing but watch and be ready in case she needed his help. She was proud and independent, and it frustrated him at times. They met in the lobby after dressing and decided to go to the diner for a cup of coffee and a slice of pie. Actually, Walter wanted pie. Lillian was content with just coffee.

The dining area was packed when they arrived, so they chose a couple of stools at the counter.

"Here are some menus. My name is Margo; just shout when you're ready."

Margo walked away and started wiping down the ketchup bottles.

"I love sitting at the counter." Lillian leaned into Walter.

"You do? How come?" Walter was studying the pie choices on the menu.

"It reminds me of when I was a little girl. My mother would take me for root beer floats. I miss her so much. To think I am a woman who's nearly ninety-two, and I still want my mother."

"I don't think that ever goes away. It's not about age. Your mom is always the one who could make everything better. That sticks with you. Especially through rough times." Walter put his glasses on. "I guess it would help if I could read the menu."

"I think you're right." Lillian grinned.

"Of course, I'm right. I'd never be able to see what the heck they have."

"No, silly. I mean, I think you're right about moms. Mine was the best. My dad was always working, and she basically took on both roles. My father disowned me when I wanted to marry a boy who wasn't up to his financial standards. But Mom would secretly come and visit us. Sometimes she'd throw an extra couple of bucks in my cookie jar. I'd never find it until she had left. Moms are smart too." She gazed past the counter.

"One time, I came home from the attorney's office ,where I took a part-time job. There must have been ten bags of groceries hidden behind the bushes. I almost didn't see them. Good thing I noticed a squirrel run across the lawn and hide under one of them.

"She knew what time I got home, so she made sure she was gone by the time I arrived. After my husband's business took off and we were comfortable, she still came by leaving money in the cookie jar. I had to hide it," Lillian laughed heartily.

"Sounds like a great woman."

"She was. I can't believe it's been over forty years since I heard her voice. Sometimes I pull out all the old photographs. She was beautiful ... both inside and out." A tear trickled down her cheek.

"Life sure does pass quickly."

"Have you picked your pie, Mr. Reilly?" Lillian glanced at the menu.

"Banana cream."

"Oh, that does sound good. I think I'll get a slice too."

"That's my girl. I'm gonna put some meat on those bones yet." Walter leaned over and tasted her lips.

"Hey, you two, am I gonna have to warn you about fraternizing in public like I do the tweens?" Margo laughed.

"We'll behave. It's just that this lady is so beautiful." Walter winked.

"You're both so cute. Are you ready to place your order?"

"Two slices of banana cream pie and a coffee refill when you have a moment." Walter handed Margo the menus.

"Coming right up." Margo smiled.

"I'm concerned about Frank." Lillian frowned.

"Frank? Have you heard something?"

"No. But he hasn't been out of the house since Elsa's funeral. Vincent told me he stopped by the other day, and the house was quiet. No television or radio was on, and Frank was sitting in the living room in the dark. Vincent stayed for a few minutes, but Frank wasn't up to conversation, so he left. I was thinking maybe we could stop by and see him tomorrow." Lillian entwined her fingers in Walter's hand.

"I think that's a good idea. Afterward, we can have lunch at my house. Does that sound alright?"

"It does. But maybe we can try to get Frank out of the house. We could come back here. He loves the food here. Remember when he used to stop and pick up those greasy grilled cheese sandwiches on the way home. Elsa would get so angry because she'd make a nice dinner for him, and he would already be full."

"I do remember that. I also remember she put a stop to it," Walter laughed.

"That she did. I miss her. She was such a sweet person."

"Me too. She and Gina were very close. When Gina passed, Elsa cooked for me every night until I moved in with Robert and Vivienne. I know it was only two blocks over, but she came every day around four-thirty. She didn't have to do that. None of you did. I remember many a day you were at my doorstep with a Tupperware container."

Lillian rested her head on his shoulder, and Walter kissed her.

The pie came, and the two sat reminiscing about some of the silly things that had happened over the years. Walter remembered the time Gina had the yen to drive. She was nearly thirty before she got the bug to learn. And Walter being Walter was a terrible teacher. He was so impatient and critical it nearly ended the marriage. They both agreed an outside service would be better if there was any future for their family.

Lillian laughed at each account of her grumpy old man.

"You were grumpy even when you were young." She stole a piece of his pie.

"Hey. What's wrong with yours?" Walter jokingly covered his plate with his hand.

"I don't know. Yours just taste better."

"You're right, you know." He held his empty cup up for the waitress.

"About?"

"Me being grumpy. I don't know how Gina dealt with me all those years."

"Because you are a good man, and she was a saint."

Walter couldn't help but laugh. Lillian had a way of taking the dark feelings and turning them around. Too bad she couldn't be there when he had the nightmares.

"Well, my dear, I'm full."

"You should be. You ate your pie and half of mine." Lillian pushed the empty plate toward the end of the counter.

"What? No, I didn't. You ate your own slice."

"I did. I ate about half before you dug in and finished it." Lillian smirked. "In your defense, I gave it to you. I slid it over when you were talking. You didn't even notice."

"Oh, so trying to get me fat, huh?"

"I like a little meat on a man's bones."

Walter rubbed his belly. "No worries here."

After he paid the check, they walked to the car. The darkness hadn't found its way to the New York sky just yet. They sat in the car and stared at the nightly show of muted gray, salmon, and pinks. The shades could be so beautiful at dusk. After a few appreciative sighs, they began discussing their plans for *mission Frank,* as Lillian called it. Since Frank was across the street from Walter, Lillian would drive over at about eleven-thirty. They would skip the pool. It pained them to give up a day when the end of their morning swims was just around the corner, but they agreed that Frank came first. They'd walk over together and coax him out to lunch.

With the solidification of Mission Frank, they drove to

Walter's house.

"No dinner tonight." Lillian patted her chest.

"You okay?" Walter's brows knitted.

"I'm fine. It seems the pie wants to make a command performance."

"Oh, so you're burping."

"Walter." Lillian's mouth hung open.

In many ways, she was still the old-fashioned woman. Certain things were not done in public, and you certainly didn't speak about them.

"I apologize. But seriously, are you feeling alright?" Walter glanced over at her.

"I'm fine. I'm going to curl up on the couch with my favorite show at ten o'clock and rest.""

"Oh yeah. Which one is that?" Walter's interest peaked.

"*Criminal Minds*. I love that kid..." Lillian took a tissue from her purse and blotted her forehead.

"Me too. I watch it all the time. There's a marathon tonight. You warm? I can lower the heat."

"Thank you. I am a bit overheated. Must be my digestion getting the best of me."

Walter set the heat on low and glanced again at her. Her skin glistened from the beads of sweat, and her color had gotten paler.

"Maybe I should take you to get looked at. There's a clinic on the way home."

"Nonsense. I don't need any more medical attention. I've had enough over the past few months to keep my doctor in a Cadillac until he's old and gray. And he's only about thirty."

"Okay. But if you don't feel well later and you need *anything*, promise you'll call me," Walter pleaded.

"I promise," Lillian ended the discussion.

The silence for the remainder of the ride home was deafening to Walter. He was worried about her, and she was clear on her stance on the matter.

Walter hated when he didn't have a choice, but he knew Lillian well enough not to test the waters. He'd wind up drowning.

As she pulled up to Walter's door, Lillian stared straight ahead. Walter inched over and took her in his arms. He caressed her back and cheek and then brushed his hand over her silken hair before he kissed her goodnight. He opened the car door and stood on the sidewalk. All he could do was watch her drive away.

Walter opened the front door, and a blast of warm air greeted him. Vivienne and Robert were sitting at the dining room table. Walter could scarcely see the wood grain finish of the table; it was covered in a collage of white envelopes.

"Hey. I thought pregnant women were always hot. This is like a volcano in here," Walter grumbled.

"Viv's cold tonight." Robert didn't look up.

"Could it be from the mountain of bills you have lying across the table?"

"Don't worry about it. Did you have a good time with Lillian and the others at the pool?" Robert checked the clock. "It's late. You stay there this whole time?"

"No. We went to the diner for pie." Walter scanned the addresses on the envelopes. All medical.

"Oh good, good. Viv didn't cook. I picked up a pizza on the way home. There are three slices on a plate in the fridge."

"Not hungry, but thank you. I may munch on them later. Is there anything I can do to help? I can give you some of my social security check. I get it on Wednesday."

"No. Thank you. Really. We appreciate it. We've got this just about figured out."

But Walter knew by the blank stare in Vivienne's eyes that Robert was just giving him lip service. They were both stressed to the limit. He didn't want to add to their plight, so he decided to watch TV in his room.

Criminals Minds was both entertainment and a distraction—usually. But Walter couldn't stop thinking about his son and daughter-in-aw drowning in an ocean of bills. When he sold the house, he had made a small profit. Just enough to be a safety net. At the time, he never imagined it would be used as a down payment on the astronomical hospital bill he had incurred when they saved his life. Since then, Robert and his brothers had been absorbing the financial burden.

It wasn't enough for Robert to bury his only child. No, he had to take on the care of his aging father as well. Walter's calm began to rise to volcanic levels as he thought about the day that had changed them all for the rest of their lives. In his dreams, there was always a sadness, an overwhelming sense of loss. As if his life was being slowly drained and the only thing left was a cold, blank shell. But in the wake of day, his sadness often floated away, leaving only rage.

He redirected his attention to the television and tried to submerge himself, but it was too late. His thoughts were wild with destruction, tearing down the happiness and blotting out any thoughts of the future.

Walter punched the side of his mattress. His fist slipped, hitting the wooden bed rail holding the head and footboard together. It wasn't until he noticed the blood smeared on his sheets that he stopped.

Stumbling to get up, he grabbed hold of the nightstand. After he washed the cuts and bandaged them, he pulled the sheets off his bed and replaced them with clean ones. He piled the soiled set into his hamper and returned to bed.

Checking the clock, he figured it was still early enough to call Lillian. He needed to hear her voice.

"Hello," Walter heard a thud.

"Walter?"

"Yes. It's me. You alright?" Walter spoke loudly.

"I am. I dropped the phone and struggled to reach it between the couch and the table. But all is well. How are you? Your voice sounds ... troubled."

"I'm having a difficult night. But I feel better just talking with you," his voice cracked.

"It's going to be alright. Everything will get better. I promise," Lillian softened her tone.

They spoke for another twenty minutes or so before agreeing to hang up. Walter could hear her yawning. He laid down in bed and turned up the volume on the TV. His body was at peace once more. Drifting off, he felt the slowing of his heart and the possibility of things to come. He smiled.

Walter woke up with a spark of vitality. He had a purpose. "Mission Frank" was a go. Lillian had called Walter early that morning, confirming the time of her arrival. They would need to be firm but kind. Coax Frank, but not push. That's what Lillian said. Walter wasn't sure what it meant, but he'd soon find out.

Eleven-thirty on the dot, the doorbell rang. Walter opened it, and there stood Lillian, in all her vim and vigor. Her bright eyes and perfect posture were a sign of life. Walter loved seeing her like this. Frank would not know what hit him.

"You ready?" She ambled toward the sidewalk.

"Whoa. Let me get my coat, woman."

Walter quickly slipped on his jacket and snatched up his cane nestled on the side of the couch. The two sauntered off across the street and right to Frank's front door.

He knocked loud enough for Frank to hear no matter where he was in the house. There wasn't an answer, so Walter peeked inside the front window. The television was on, and the house was dark, just as Vincent had described it.

Walter pounded again. This time, he heard some rumbling coming from the back of the house followed by the thumping of heavy footsteps. They heard the lock unlatch, and he scooted back next to Lillian.

Frank opened the door and squinted.

"Frank. How are you?" Lillian stepped closer to him.

"Uh. Fine... fine. What brings you two here today?"

"Well, you, of course. May we come in?"

Frank reluctantly agreed and stepped aside to let them enter.

There was a half-eaten buttered roll on a TV tray with a cup of black coffee and a folded copy of the local newspaper. Walter and Lillian sat on the couch, and Frank took a seat in his recliner. He turned the volume down on the television and switched on the light next to his chair.

Walter's eyes caught a mess of clothes piled in the corner of the room with a laundry basket sitting beside them. The end table contained a white film of thick dust, and there was a pile of dirty dishes on the dining room table, clearly visible through the archway that separated the rooms. His heart began to race when he realized the most disturbing thing about the room was set on top of the side table next to Frank's recliner.

A black Glock semi-automatic nine-millimeter handgun. His hands clammed up, and he took off his coat to fend off the sweat that was beading around his neck from the anxiety.

Not wanting to alarm Lillian, Walter asked Frank if he could get a cup of coffee.

"Sure. You like it black?" Frank got up.

"Yes. Thank you," Walter rubbed his palms on his pants.

"Lillian, would you like a cup?" Frank asked.

"Thank you. I would. Let me help you."

Lillian started to stand up, but Walter tugged at her arm.

"No. You stay. I'll go help him." Walter quickly rose.

The two men went into the kitchen. Frank took two gray mugs from the cabinet. The coffee was on the warmer, and he filled the mugs nearly to the top. Walter stopped him when he tried to pick one of them up.

"How are you feeling, my friend?" Walter took a sip from one of the mugs.

"Fine. Good," Frank sounded impatient.

"Good. And the Glock sitting in your living room?"

"What about it?" Frank snapped.

"Why is it there? You plan on doing some target practice?"

Frank was an expert marksman. In his younger days, he participated in several shooting competitions. His guns were normally kept safe under lock and key.

"Yeah. I'm going to go this afternoon."

"I'll go with you. I haven't been out to the range in months. What time is your shoot?"

"Two o'clock. I booked the range for only one. Maybe next time." Frank nervously fidgeted with his hands.

"Which range? The one on Fifth and Haven?"

"Yup." Frank rocked back and forth.

"Oh, great. I know Stan, the owner. We go way back. There won't be a problem. This is great. We came over to take you to lunch. Lillian has her heart set on the cheeseburger at the diner. She's so funny. Sometimes she gets a taste for the most unexpected things. Anyway, we'll have lunch, and then you and me can go to the range."

Frank stood there, mouth wide open. Walter watched as he struggled to get the words out.

"Uh ... no. I'm not in the mood for lunch. I just ate breakfast. You know, I think I'm gonna cancel my appointment too. I'm feeling a little tired today. We can go another day."

"Nonsense. It will do you good to get out. You've been cooped up in this house for far too long. Do you think Elsa would want this for you? Besides, there's no way you're changing the mind of the little lady sitting in the living room. When she gets an idea in her head, it's better to just go along with it."

"Hey, what are you two doing in here?" Lillian was standing in the doorway. "I could have gone to Columbia and picked the beans myself by now."

"We're coming. I was just telling Frank that after lunch, we'll go to the shooting range."

"That's a good idea. I've been wanting to get some shopping done so I'll stay in town. This works out perfectly."

Frank stood there with no expression on his face. He rubbed his hands a few times before halfheartedly agreeing. Walter knew it was Lillian that had swayed him. If she hadn't come in when she had, the conversation would have ended up differently. Frank clearly wasn't going just because

Walter insisted. It took the persuasion of another kind to get him to agree.

They agreed it was easier to take two cars. Otherwise, they would have to come back for Frank's Hyundai, which would inconvenience Lillian and her plans to do some afternoon shopping.

On the way to the diner, Walter voiced his concerns for his friend to Lillian. Never mentioning the gun, he used Frank's mood and the condition of the house as reasoning for his thoughts.

"Do you think it's more serious than Vincent had thought?" Lillian kept her eyes on the road.

"I do. But if we can talk to him and keep him company, maybe we can snap him out of it. We have a few more weeks left at the pool. I think we should try and get him to come." Walter partially rolled down his window.

"I think that's a marvelous idea. If we can get him together with everybody, I bet it will lift his spirits." Lillian grinned.

"I think Ryan might be able to help us. The boy's pretty persuasive."

"What do you mean?"

"He's the one that convinced me to start going."

"Well, I'm glad he did."

"Me too."

Walter brushed his hand over hers. Lillian squeezed it, gently intertwining their fingers. It was going to be a struggle today, and he wouldn't want to do it without her.

When they reached the diner, Frank was still right behind them. They pulled in and parked next to each other in the first two open spaces.

Luckily there were plenty of booths open, and the hostess seated them in one near the windows.

Walter knew how much Lillian preferred a window seat, so he waited as she scooted in. Frank sat across from them and concentrated on the menu. There was a senior selection on the back, but he never looked at it. Instead, he went right to the lunch specials.

"They never have the best selection for the senior choices." Frank adjusted his glasses.

"I know what you mean. They think all we eat is plain hamburgers, meatloaf, and spaghetti. For once, I'd like to see a T-bone and baked potato offered." Walter shook his head.

"Well, I'm having a thick cheeseburger with steak fries and a salad." Lillian beamed.

The two men looked at her tiny little self and laughed.

"No dessert?" Walter chimed.

"Oh, I'm thinking about it."

"It's good to see you with a healthy appetite again." Walter kissed her.

"I'm happy you found each other. I know you were having a hard time after Gina passed, Walter. Lillian, how long has it been since Sam's accident?"

"Thirty-four years. I lost him young."

"You've been alone too long," Walter declared.

"It has been a very long time." She glanced out toward the other customers in the diner. "He was a good man. The stars took him too quickly."

Walter's brows furrowed, and his lips pursed. "The stars?" his tone was curt.

Lillian's attention was abruptly averted from the strangers to her friend.

"Yes, the stars. Why? Is something wrong with what I said?"

"Well, shouldn't you have said God took him too soon?"

"No. I said what I meant."

Walter was at a crossroads. He loved spending time with Lillian. Over the past several weeks, his feelings for her had grown tremendously. But he and Gina were Catholics. No, he didn't go to church. Yes, he was mad as hell at God, but none of that meant he didn't believe. He wasn't quite sure how to handle an intimate relationship with someone who thought the *stars* had anything to do with life and death. His belly was on fire, and the heat rose into his chest. His agitation had taken hold of his reasoning and replaced his happiness toward her with a cold black hole of doubt.

"Do we have a problem, Walter?" With her elbows on the table, Lillian leaned into him.

"Wait, the two of you stop this crap right now. Who cares what either of you believes? You have each other. At the end of the day, when the house is silent because you're all alone, do you really think any of this matters? Walter, if you can't let this go, and it costs you Lillian, well, my friend, you are the biggest fool I have ever met."

Walter couldn't let it go. It went against everything he had based his life on. He had to believe there was a heaven and that Chase was there, happy and waiting for the day his family could join him.

He envisioned him with Gina, holding her hand. They were in the presence of our Lord and would be loved for all eternity.

That is what he held on to. Anger with God did strain his belief in the beginning, but he realized his anger didn't change what was true.

He studied the lines on Lillian's face. They were gentle for her age, and her eyes still twinkled with a wonder for life. *Am I really that unwilling to choose a compromise?*

"This is very difficult for me. Chase..." he couldn't finish the sentence.

Lillian placed her hand on his forearm.

"I understand, Walter. You need this. But it doesn't mean that I don't need to believe the things I do. It certainly doesn't change how I feel toward you. It has so little to do with our relationship."

His anger subsided to a warm heat.

"Can we let this discussion go?" he pleaded.

"We can." Lillian moved her hand off of his arm.

The silence was excruciating. For the first time since they had been together, it felt awkward. The food came, and there was barely a word spoken. They were certainly failing at lifting Frank up from his depression. The heaviness was pushing down on them, and Walter wondered if he could ever recapture what he once had with Lillian.

Despite it all, they stuck to the plan. After they were finished eating, Lillian went her own way, and the guys headed to the range. Walter welcomed the *pow, pow* of the streaming bullets. At first, there was hesitation, but after Frank let off a few rounds, Walter jumped in with both feet.

The gun felt comfortable in his hand, almost comforting. He had control when he was holding a firearm.

He chose when and when not to shoot. The powerful force he felt surging through his body gave him a sense of empowerment he knew how to harness.

In the past, whenever he did go to the range, he would often find himself observing the other shooters. Some of them were very young and clearly did not have respect for the weapon they were firing. They thought it was a game among friends. Their boisterous comments and loud yelling when making a shot was a glimpse into the future and a possible sad ending.

He'd seen it happen more than once. A group of inexperienced guys would go out shooting in the woods and wind up carrying a lifeless body back. They were under the assumption that one lesson and a shiny new toy gave them all they needed to play cops and robbers. But the game that they were playing was not a game at all. It was a real gun with real bullets that, once they pierced your flesh, took away your very real life. Video games and movies desensitized the culture so much, giving birth to an entire generation who fought wars in their living room.

Walter shook his head and tried to drown out the yelps from the wet-behind-the-ears squadron of military wannabees. He took aim, and with expert precision, shot his loaner forty-five. Walter preferred the old fashion revolver over the semi-automatic that was Frank's weapon of choice. He pulled the target back—three shots to the head and two to the heart. *If only I had my gun that day.*

Walter changed out the black silhouette with a new one and sent it sailing backward. He raised his pistol and shot off a continuous round of bullets until his gun was empty. He reloaded and then repeated.

He reloaded and then repeated again. He was about to do it yet again when he felt a hand reach for his arm and hold it tightly to his side. Frank was standing next to him, shaking his head.

"Put the gun down. I think we're finished for today." Frank took the pistol from his hands.

Walter stood there, unable to move. His chest barely pumping, he couldn't catch his breath. Sweat beaded across his forehead and upper lip. He could taste the salt.

"Come on. Let's go." Frank grabbed his friend's arm and led him to the counter to return the gun.

When the transaction was complete, they got in the car. Frank waited a moment to start the engine. Walter sat looking straight ahead, his seatbelt unbuckled.

"Walter. Belt up."

Walter didn't move.

"Buddy. We can't go anywhere until you're belted." Frank gripped the steering wheel.

"I could have saved him—them. If I had my gun with me. I could have done something."

"What? Do you think you're some kind of superhero? You know what happened. It wouldn't have made a difference."

"How could you say that? I could have gotten shots out, and those people and our Chasey would be here today," Walter's voice raised in anger.

Frank looked at him and then gazed out of the windshield.

"Put on your seatbelt."

He waited for a response. Walter looked over at Frank, grabbed his belt, and clicked himself into safety.

When they pulled up Frank's driveway, Walter got out and walked across the street to his house. He didn't even bother talking to Ryan, who was out front taking out the garbage.

He went inside, took off his coat, and went straight to his room. Still worried about Frank, he had to let it go. There was nothing left inside to give today. Taking off his shoes, he laid down on his bed and closed his eyes. It was too bright. Struggling to get up, he hobbled to the window and shut the blinds before collapsing once again onto the overstuffed comforter. He needed to take a nap and let sleep wash away the horror in his mind and the events of the day. The dream world brought him to the evil that changed their lives. Only this time, he was prepared.

Chapter Seventeen

Days went by, and Walter didn't hear anything from Lillian. She was not at the pool, and he was too stubborn to reach out. He did, however, go over to Frank's every morning before Vivienne drove him to the Community Center. His attempts were well thought out but unsuccessful. Frank remained aloof.

When Walter entered the swimming area, he was surprised to see Lillian sitting on one of the lounges speaking with Evelyn. He wanted to go to her, but he had something he had to take care of first. Ryan was with Grace at the edge of the pool. They were conducting a beginning swim class for a few of the seniors.

"Walter, what's going on today? You here to take our class?"

"Nope. But there is something I wanted to talk to you about if you have a moment?" Walter tried not to look obvious as he glanced over at Lillian.

"Sure. Give me a second."

Ryan whispered something to Grace, and she nodded her head.

"Okay. Let's go over here and sit down." Ryan pointed to a couple of empty lifeguard chairs.

"You know Frank Taylor from across the street, right?" Walter sat back and folded his arms.

"Yes, I do. It was sad about Mrs. Taylor. She was so nice."

"I'm concerned about him, and I've been trying to get him to come here, but he won't budge. I thought maybe you could talk to him."

"Sure. There are only a few weeks left, though."

"I know. But I still think it might do him some good. What do you say?"

"I'll talk to him tonight when I get home. Do you want to come with me?"

"No. I think he's sick of seeing me, and besides, you need to get him alone to work your magic like you did with me."

Ryan laughed and nodded his head in agreement. After they spoke for a few more minutes, Ryan excused himself and went back to the class.

Walter peered over his left shoulder, attempting to get another glimpse of Lillian. She was gone.

"Why do you keep looking over there when I'm right next to you?"

Walter jumped. He hadn't seen her come around and sit down.

"What do you mean? What makes you think I was looking for you?" Walter sounded defensive.

"I see we're still in the same bad place. Never mind, Mr. Reilly. Enjoy your swim."

Lillian stood up to leave, but Walter clasped his hand around her forearm. Startled, she nearly lost her balance and quickly stood up and steadied herself.

"Please. Sit down so that we can talk."

"I am too old and tired to be treated like this. I like you, Walter. I really do. But I am not the punching bag for your angry innuendos." Lillian sat.

"I know. You're right. I'm sorry. I shouldn't have attacked you like that. What you believe is up to you." Walter struggled with the words. "My life has been more lows than highs over the past few years. I took my struggles with my faith out on you.

It's so hard to hold on to everything you've been taught your whole life when the very thing that was supposed to be there in times of need— wasn't.

"I prayed so hard that day," he continued. "Pulled out all the cards and set them on the table. I promised if he would just get Chase and the others through this, I would do better. Go to church every Sunday and be a better person. Lillian, I begged him, pleaded for him to take me. I'm old. I've had a life. But my Chasey, he was just getting started. For Christ's sake, his biggest worry was that his mom packed potato chips in his lunch instead of pretzels. Where the hell was the Almighty that day? I am so angry I could spit.

"I don't want to lose you too. I can't. You're the reason I get up and come here every day."

Walter's tears trickled down his cheeks.

Lillian softly wiped them away with the back of her hand. "I understand. But that doesn't make it right. I am here; your friends are here to help. If you would just let us in instead of fighting it. Knowing you can pick up a phone, come here or meet for coffee at the diner, that's what we hold on to. We can move on from here if you are willing to accept our differences and embrace our friendship." Lillian pressed her lips together and took a deep breath.

Walter clasped her hand and brought it up to his lips. "I can." He stood up and extended his hand.

They walked hand in hand to the pool and immersed themselves in the swaying aqua blue and wonderful circle of friends. The day was light and happy, and for the first time in what seemed to be forever, Walter actually enjoyed being surrounded by people.

That evening Walter took Lillian to the diner, where they met up with Vincent, Norman, Harry, and Evelyn. He tried desperately to stay focused, but all he could think about was Ryan's impending conversation with Frank.

Finding the loaded gun on the table the other day nearly stopped his heart. He had been friends with Frank and Elsa for so many years. Frank was never a quitter. The thought that he could even contemplate ending his own life horrified Walter beyond belief. And although he didn't have confirmation that it was, without a doubt, his intentions, his strange behavior that day gave support to Walter's fear.

"Hey, where are you tonight?" Lillian was tapping his thigh.

"Huh. Oh, I'm sorry." Walter refocused on his friends.

"Vincent was asking you how Vivienne is feeling." Lillian took a sip of tea.

"Yes. I heard the good news. Is she getting along okay?" Vincent inquired.

"As far as I can tell, she's doing fine. Viv tells me the mornings are the hardest, but it seems to have settled down. I haven't seen any green face for about a week."

"Oh, that's great news. Tell her I send my best, would you?" Vincent's flashed a wide grin.

"I will. Thank you. I know she'll appreciate it."

"So, gents and lovely Lillian, what shall we do after we eat? Anyone up for a movie?"

The group stared at Norman.

"I don't think we thought about an after-dinner adventure, but it sounds good to me." Lillian stole Walter's cherry from atop his sundae. "What do you say, you old geezer, want to go see a movie?"

"Old geezer? I'm full of energy; bring it on." Walter puffed his chest.

"Careful. You'll hurt yourself," Vincent chimed in.

"Hey. She can talk to me like that, not you." Walter made a fist.

"Yeah. Yeah. Just be careful you don't hit yourself with that," Vincent laughed.

By the end of dinner, only four had agreed to a movie. Evelyn was growing tired, still on the mend from the accident, and Harry took her home to rest. Walter and Lillian piled in her car, and Vincent and Norman followed behind them. They were only about ten minutes away from the Hanover Theater. It was the oldest movie house in the neighborhood. Walter wasn't sure how it escaped the recent deaths of all the local oldies, but somehow it was still standing.

The Hanover Theater still showcased the red velvet drapes that opened up before each movie began, revealing the giant screen. There was only one screen, a reminiscence of days long gone. The theater was playing an oldie but goodie, and the gang was thrilled.

A Streetcar Named Desire was a favorite of Lillian's, and it was one of Gina's too.

Walter ordered a large popcorn, large soda, and a box of candy. Lillian pinched him when he put too much salt on the popcorn.

"Hey. That hurt."

"Not as much as that salt you're pouring by the gallon on that popcorn."

Walter went to snap back but retracted. He liked having a woman worry about him again.

"Okay, let me see if I can blot some of it off." Walter grabbed some napkins. "There; it's good."

Lillian reached in, grabbed a handful, and popped it in her mouth. "Surprisingly enough, it is."

"How the hell can the two of you even think of eating popcorn and candy after the dinner and dessert we all had?" Norman leaned forward to see Walter.

"You can't go to the theater and not get popcorn. It's practically sacrilegious," Walter retorted.

Norman rolled his eyes and sat back.

The theater darkened. The show was about to start. Walter tingled with excitement. Even though he saw the film a dozen times, each time was like the first when sitting in front of the big screen. He heard Lillian rummaging through her purse, and he leaned in.

"Is there something I can get you?" He waited, but she didn't respond.

Her search became more agitated, and Walter carefully turned her head and cupped her chin.

Lillian had a stream of blood pouring from her left nostril. He grabbed her purse and practically dumped everything out before he found her tissues.

"Walter, it won't stop."

"Here you go. It's going to be alright. Put your head back." Walter put his sweater behind her head.

"What's going on?" Vincent had scooted forward.

"Lillian has a nosebleed."

He turned back to Lillian. The tissue was soaked with blood, and it was streaming down her face and neck.

"Walter..." Lillian's voice trembled.

"Vincent, please call emergency services."

He nodded and pulled his phone from his pocket.

The staff must have heard their commotion because two young gentlemen came over to check on them. When they realized what was happening, they stopped the film and brought up the lights. Lillian began crying, and Walter did his best to calm her down. He wadded up a stack of napkins and held it to her nose. Blood was everywhere. He drew her in close and tilted her head slightly back.

"It's gonna be okay. We'll go, and the doctors will fix everything," Walter spoke softly.

Lillian began to shake. He increased the pressure of both the napkins and his hug, but it did little to stop her fears. By the time the paramedics arrived, she was sobbing uncontrollably.

Walter was nudged to the side while experienced hands did their work. In minutes she was loaded into the ambulance with Walter riding next to her.

The paramedic told them they were going to Our Lady of Saints Catholic Hospital. Vincent and Norman told him they'd meet him there. He asked if they would please call Viv and Robert to let them know.

Walter's heart ran a race with his anxiety. But he didn't care. He was too worried about Lillian. She had drifted in and out of consciousness. Judging by the conversation he heard between the two paramedics, it wasn't good.

As they worked to stabilize Lillian, Walter spoke to her. He wasn't sure if she had heard him, but he wanted her to know he hadn't left her.

Within minutes they reached the ER, and she was whisked in. Walter wasn't family, so he had to stay in the waiting room. He immediately started to pace. This was the place he hated the most. Anger, grief, and worry bubbled to the surface as he choked back the tears.

Thankfully, Vincent and Norman arrived about ten minutes later.

"Walter, do you know how to contact her niece?" Norman paced around the room.

"No. I don't have any of her family's contact information."

"Oh, no. What about that Ryan kid?" Norman kept pacing.

"What about him?"

"Didn't you say he had been helping her out? You know, groceries occasionally, that sort of thing. Maybe he knows something," Norman questioned.

Oh, Walter knew things too. He knew Lillian had been battling bone cancer and treatment sometimes made her ill to the point that she stopped it. He knew she didn't stand a chance without it. He knew this could be the beginning of her end. And he knew he wasn't ready.

"I'll call him." Walter took out his phone. "And please, Norman, sit down. You're making me dizzy."

Ryan had just gotten back from his visit with Frank. He thought it had gone well ,and Frank agreed to come to the center in the morning. Then Walter hit him with the news. There was a span of silence before Ryan relayed the phone number to Lillian's niece, Barbara. She was her emergency contact.

Walter thanked him and hung up. He immediately called Barbara and explained what had happened. Barbara lived several towns over but would leave immediately. Given the time of day, traffic wouldn't be an issue. Still, it would be a few hours before she could get there.

The emergency room was large, but there wasn't enough seating to accommodate all the families and patients stuck in the waiting room limbo. Some of those waiting had taken to the floor. Walter desperately needed a cup of coffee. His throat had been dry and tight since watching Lillian being wheeled away.

The reception nurse directed them to the vending machines down the hall. Norman and Vincent made the run.

Walter looked around at the drab gray walls and burgundy floral chairs. There was nothing about the room that was comfortable. It was cold, and the fluorescent lighting did little to brighten the place. It did succeed, however, in making the sick look even worse. Their pasty color was accented by the white glare.

"Here you go, buddy." Norman handed Walter a Styrofoam cup filled with black comfort.

"Thanks. Where's Vincent?" Walter inquired. "You're not going to believe this. He ran into a nurse he knows. I guess she has the swing shift. She'll be getting off soon. But she's going to check on Lillian for us. He's waiting in the hall until she gets back."

"Really? Oh, thank God. At least we'll hear something. I was hoping we didn't have to wait for Barbara to get here."

"Yeah. I know what you mean. Hopefully, we'll get some good news."

The clock on the wall above the reception window read ten forty-five. They had been there for forty-five minutes already. Walter shuddered when he thought back on the last time he was in the hospital. It was when Elsa fell ill. He thought of how different she had looked, laying in the hospital bed hooked up to every tube imaginable. Doctor Frankenstein had nothing on modern medicine. For all their accomplishments, however, they couldn't make a damn decent cup of coffee. He winced when he took another sip.

His thoughts were interrupted when Vincent came barreling through the double doors separating them from the hospital corridor. He took a seat between Walter and Norman. His heavy brows and tight mouth gave an insight into the news before he uttered a word.

"It's not good. They're trying to stabilize her, but the bleeding won't stop. She's not conscious, which I guess right now is a good thing," Vincent sat back and took a sip of coffee. "God, this is the worst cup of coffee I've ever had. Kathie, my nurse friend, said she'll check one more time before she leaves. She'll come and find us with any updates before she leaves."

Walter swallowed hard. It was difficult to control the shakiness in his voice. "Did she say why they think they can't get the bleeding under control?"

"It has something to do with the chemo she's been getting. Did you know she was sick? I was shocked when Kathie said chemo."

"Chemo?" Norman chimed in.

Walter sat quietly. He didn't want to lie to his friends, but he didn't want to betray Lillian's confidence either. "I knew. But she wasn't ready to share with anyone else."

"How long have you known?" Vincent asked.

"It doesn't matter. The important thing right now is Lillian. What are they doing to stop it?" his voice cracked.

"Kathie didn't say. I'll ask her when she comes back. Is it serious? I mean, of course, it's serious if she's getting chemo. But is it fixable or—manageable?"

"My understanding is, it's manageable. There is nothing they can do to cure her. I think the chemo is just to give her more time. But I'm not so sure it's better. She's had some hard times." He didn't mention her recent choice to stop the treatment.

"You know, I thought there might be something up. She's missed a lot of days at the Center this year, and sometimes, when she'd come, she would be so quiet and just lay down on one of the chaises. I thought it might be her arthritis, but I never imagined cancer. That is what we are talking about, right?" Vincent's voice trailed.

Walter nodded his head in agreement. In his mind, it wasn't a boundary crossing if he didn't initiate or further the conversation.

"When did Barbara say she should be here?" Vincent inquired.

"She said it would take her a few hours. I spoke to her around ten—ten-fifteen. I figure she should get here sometime around one or one-thirty. There should be no traffic, so I think it will be clear sailing on the parkway."

"Kathie should be here soon. She got off at eleven and had some paperwork to do for the shift change. She said it could take about half an hour. After that, she was going to check on Lillian again." Vincent got up and threw his coffee in the trash.

"Walter. I get that you don't want to talk about what's going on with Lillian, but do you think Barbara will let us know?" Vincent sat down.

"Yeah. This being in the dark just makes it worse." Norman crossed his arms.

"I know how you both are feeling; I really do. I've been with her for the past few months, not once being able to discuss it with her. On the bad days, I have to *pretend* it's the flu or something she ate that disagreed with her. Believe me, it hasn't been easy. I knew she would tell me when she was ready. The time hasn't come for her yet to share. And there were days that she was so ill, I was afraid we'd lose her, and the words would never be said," Walter stuttered on the last sentence.

"What words?" Norman leaned over to hear him better.

"What?"

"You said 'the words would never be said.' What words?" Norman yawned.

"I don't know what I'm saying. I'm exhausted," Walter brushed him off.

The room started to thin out, and the empty seats had all the makings of a modern-day horror flick. One by one, they all disappeared. Taken by a serial killer hiding in the walls of the hospital ever since he lost his wife to a mistake made by a surgeon thirty years ago. First, he had taken the doctor and slit his throat. He buried him beneath the new construction for the left wing dedicated to the cardiac unit. He continued his killing spree, sporadically taking victims from the ER over decades, their bodies never to be found. *I need to stop watching those late-night B movies on cable,* thought Walter.

"Walter, I'm going to get some chips from the vending machine. Would you like something?" Vincent was standing in front of him.

"I think I'd like a Hershey bar, if they have it. What about Norman?"

Walter glanced over to Norman who was lightly snoring with his head tilted back on the chair, and his arms crossed in front of his chest.

"He likes Paydays. I'll get him one. Let him sleep. And yes, they do have Hershey's. I saw them when I went for the coffee," Vincent grabbed his jacket. "It's damn cold in those hallways."

"Wait. What if your nurse friend comes? I don't know what she looks like."

"Oh, it's okay. She has to pass by the vending machines to get here. I'll see her." Vincent zipped his jacket.

"Oh. Great." Walter managed a forced smile.

The temperature in the room had dropped as well. Walter draped his sweater over his chest and pulled it up to his neck. Norman's low hum became a nasal trumpet. Walter shook him slightly. Luckily, he quieted down without waking up. *Lucky bastard,* Walter thought. *He can fall asleep anywhere.*

For as long as they had known each other, Norman always had the gift of sleep. Or at least that's how Walter viewed it. No matter where they were or what position, Norman would be out in minutes.

He reflected on one instance when they went to the city for the Christmas show at Radio City Music Hall. The subway was packed, and it was standing room only. Norman fell asleep while holding on to the safety strap that hung from the interior roof of the train. Swaying back and forth, he was bumped several times by strangers, but it never disturbed his slumber. Of course, it did have its drawbacks. One night, he fell asleep on the bus and rode it until it stopped at the bus yard. He had to call Walter to come and get him.

Vincent returned with candy bars in both fists. He handed Walter a Hershey bar and a bag of M&M's. He laid a Payday and peanut M&M's in Norman's lap.

"I didn't see Kathie. She should be coming soon. It's eleven-thirty already." Vincent tore open his bag of chips.

"Remember the time Norman fell asleep on the downtown bus and rode it all the way back to the yard? He called me in such a panic. I couldn't stop laughing." Walter took a bite of chocolate.

"Yeah. And then you got lost picking him up. He called me wondering where the hell you were," Vincent chortled. "The guy is a rock when it comes to sleep. I wish I could get that deep. I hear everything. It's a wonder I got any sleep at all when I lived in Brooklyn."

"I forgot you lived in Brooklyn. How long was that?" Walter asked. "Three, four years?" Walter unwrapped his bar in the paper.

"Five years. It was a blast. Except for the nightly hum of sirens and beeping of horns." He grinned.

"I can't remember why you came back to the Island?"

"Madeline."

"That's right. Boy, she was a real looker."

"You better believe it. She hated the city. When we met, she was visiting her aunt, who lived across the street from me. Her home was on the Island, and she wouldn't consider moving to the city. So, I moved back. It was really good for a while. But we eventually realized we were two very different people. It's a shame. I thought we were going to make a life together. I had even bought an engagement ring." Vincent crinkled up the empty chip bag.

"I never knew you were that close to marriage."

"Yup. She was the closest I had ever come to tying the knot. Ah, I guess it wasn't in the cards."

"Do you ever regret it?" Walter stood to stretch his legs.

"No. We weren't right for each other. She met this great guy. They have five kids, and I don't know how many grandkids. She's happy." Vincent ran his fingers through his hair.

"I meant never marrying anyone."

"You can't miss what you never had. I'm good."

Walter saw a pretty brunette in a nurse's scrubs come through the double doors and head straight for them. Vincent got up and met her halfway.

"Kathie!" Vincent kissed her cheek.

Walter got up and shook Norman to wake him. The candy bars fell on the floor and Walter picked them up and handed them to him. Joining Vincent, Walter held his breath in anticipation of bad news.

"They've stopped the bleeding, but she's still not conscious. They're going to be moving her to a room in ICU. The doctor is waiting for her family to arrive. Do you know when they'll get here?"

Walter chimed in. "Her niece should be here around one or so. Can we see her?" He felt anxious.

"No. I'm sorry, family only right now. If they wish to bring you in when they get here, that's a different story. But for now, they won't let you. I won't lie; given her present state, this is very serious. I'm so sorry."

Kathie said her goodbyes, and Vincent walked her to her car in the lot.

Walter sat quietly in his chair. He had known Lillian had stopped treatment, but he thought they'd have more time.

Vincent came back and sat down. Walter glared at the clock on the wall—it was midnight. Another hour or so and Barbara would be there. Although he wasn't sure what else they could find out, maybe she would let them go in and at least see Lillian. He couldn't bear the thought of something happening without him by her side.

Barbara arrived close to one o'clock in the morning. She recognized Walter, although they had never met. "My aunt described you to perfection, Mr. Reilly."

"Please call me Walter. This is Vincent and Norman."

"How's she doing? Have they told you anything?" Barbara's eyes were bloodshot.

"No. They wouldn't tell us because we aren't family. But Vincent knows one of the nurses, and the last we heard, they stopped the bleeding and are waiting to place her in a room in ICU." Walter brushed his hand over his mouth.

"Okay. Let me see what I can find out." Barbara approached the reception desk. She was only there a minute when the doors opened to the emergency area. "They're letting me go back. She doesn't have a room yet. I'll be back and give you an update." She slipped through the wide opening of the electronic doors and disappeared as they sealed shut.

"Waiting again." Norman stretched.

"At least now we have a connection. Barbara seemed nice," Vincent chimed.

Walter listened to them, but he wasn't as optimistic as Vincent. Seeing Lillian wouldn't make the situation better, although that was his main priority. His sadness weighed on him. Every movement required concentration. He pushed to function, and his nerves were on the edge of breaking.

There had been so much tragedy around him. Every time he had an ounce of happiness, it was snatched away like a tornado rolling in and causing devastating destruction. His strength was not only drained, but it was also giving up. He didn't want this life anymore.

Walter's thoughts were interrupted by Barbara. "Okay, I can take one of you in at a time." She darted her eyes from one guy to the other.

"Walter." Vincent and Norman said in unison.

"I guess you're it, Walter. Let's go. She's in and out of consciousness, but she'll know you're there."

"Have they stabilized her?" Walter quickened his pace.

"Yes. My aunt is a tough little cookie. I think she surprised even the doctors."

They walked down a long hallway of divided patients. There were no doors because this was the ER, the limbo before you got a room or were discharged. Curtains did offer a barrier of privacy between the patients, though. In the middle of the hall was the nurses' station and doctors' hangout.

Barbara abruptly stopped in front of space number twelve. The curtain was drawn, hiding its contents. She pulled it partially open and slipped through, waving Walter to follow. Lillian was covered with a purple blanket, and her eyes were closed. The room was barely large enough for the two to maneuver around the hospital bed.

A chair on the left side was pushed into the corner, and a bedside table and additional chair were on the right side. The heart monitor beeped, showing the update of Lillian's heart rate, and a pulse oximeter was attached to her right index finger, showing the amount of oxygen in her blood.

Anything above ninety was a plus, but ideally, high nineties were preferred. Lillian's was eighty-eight. Tubes were in her nostrils, administering life-sustaining oxygen.

Walter froze. It brought back memories of Gina's last days with her illness. He had learned much of the medical significance of each type of machinery that kept her alive—something he would have opted to have never known.

Lillian's body was lost in the bed. Her color was pasty gray, and her usually silky and shiny hair was matted to the pillow.

Walter took a seat on the right side next to the bed. He reached out and stroked her hair; it was damp. "It's freezing in this room. I wonder why she is sweating?"

"I'm not sure. The doctor is supposed to come back in before they take her to a room. I'll ask him." Barbara pulled back the curtain slightly aside to peek out into the hallway.

Walter wanted to shout, *Wake up!* Maybe shake her until she opened her eyes, but he knew those things were just images in his head. Shouting would do no good, and shaking her would only result in more pain. Her frailness scared him more than he was expecting. He tried to push out the melancholy scenarios from his mind. He couldn't. Instead, he grabbed hold of them and elaborated until it was clear there was no happy ending. Immersed deep in his own self-inflicted pain, he was startled when Lillian let out a groan.

"Little lady, we're here. Your niece, Barbara, came all the way from Montauk." Walter waited. "Lillian. Do you hear me?" He held her hand.

"Auntie. It's me, Barbara. Open your eyes. Can you do that?" Barbara soothed.

Lillian stirred again, letting out a series of whispers.

Walter moved closer to hear what she was trying to say. "You're in the hospital. Do you remember having the nosebleed at the theater?" Walter gently squeezed her hand.

She slowly nodded.

"Are you thirsty? Would you like a sip of water?" Again, Lillian nodded.

Walter searched the room, but there was no water. Barbara went to the nurse's station to ask for help. She returned with a nurse who began checking Lillian's vital signs.

"Hello, Mrs. Grainger. Do you know where you are?" The nurse was loud and clear.

Lillian turned her face toward the nurse.

"Can you talk to me? I'd like to hear that voice of yours."

"The hospi—tal," Lillian's voice was shaky.

"Good. You're thirsty?" The nurse adjusted the oxygen tubing.

"Yes." Lillian cleared her throat.

"Okay, I'll get you some ice chips to suck on."

"Ice chips? She's thirsty. Give her a glass of water," Walter demanded.

"Docs orders. No drinking until they get the rest of the test results back." The nurse left.

When she returned, she held a tall Styrofoam cup filled with ice and a spoon. She set it down on the bedside table and then positioned the table in front of Lillian. She then raised the head of the bed so it would be easier to munch on the ice.

Walter took hold of the cup and spoon and dug in, removing a small amount of ice. He carefully put the spoon to Lillian's lips. Shaking, she opened her mouth and took in the soothing coolness. She smiled. Walter's heart skipped a beat with excitement. Finally—signs of life.

Nearly two hours later, the doctor finally came in and confirmed what Walter had suspected all along. Since stopping the chemo treatment, Lillian's body was beginning to shut down. Even knowing the inevitable, he didn't think it would be this quickly.

By morning, a schedule had been set up between the guys for Lillian's visits. Barbara took the role of a permanent fixture throughout the night. At seven-thirty, medical staff took Lillian to her room. During the night, her improvement downgraded her to the Step-Down Unit, or SDU, rather than the original ICU.

Walter was pleased to hear this. She was improving enough to be lucid most of the time. She had begun to get her appetite back, which, in his book, was always a good sign.

Over the next few days, he went to the hospital every morning and stayed until visiting hours were over. There were only a couple of days left at the pool, and they were having an ending bash for all the seniors. Walter was hoping Lillian might be better in time to attend.

On the fourth day, she was well enough to be released. Barbara brought her home with Walter's help. Once Lillian was settled, Barbara took a much-needed trip to the grocery store. When she returned, Walter swore she had bought one of everything in the store. It was too far for Barbara to commute back and forth every day. She had decided to stay the rest of the week until Walter volunteered.

He convinced her it was silly to be away from her family when he had nothing but time to give. He promised daily updates and conversations when Lillian was feeling better.

With some hesitation, Barbara agreed.

The following two days went by smoothly. Walter made sure Lillian had an ample supply of food before each pain medication and tried to get her up and moving a bit by taking her on short walks through the house. When she was able, they extended their terrain to the front of the house and halfway up the block.

It was only three days away from the senior pool bash, and Lillian was growing anxious. She didn't want to miss it. Feeling stronger and managing her pain, she decided to go to the pool in the morning for a test run.

Walter objected, but he didn't stand a chance. She had made up her mind. He had tried to reason with her by asking that she wait for the actual party, but his words fell on deaf ears. He asked Vivienne for a ride, and she picked them up at nine a.m. the next day.

Worried about Lillian getting too cold, he over-packed. There was a heavy sweater, a lighter one, and a windbreaker. Lillian laughed kindheartedly when she saw the stuffed bag.

They walked into the Center hand in hand, and much to their surprise, a pack of waiting friends. Walter had mentioned to Vincent that they were coming, and apparently, it went down the senior pipeline like a wildfire. Literally just about everybody they knew was there.

Lillian beamed. The sparkle in her eyes reassured Walter this was the right decision.

They sat on the steps in the shallow end of the pool, surrounded by friends. Walter checked the electronic board; the water was a lovely seventy-eight degrees.

"How you doing, old girl?" Harry was treading water.

"Don't say that to her!" Evelyn splashed him.

"It's fine, Evelyn. He's just an old geezer himself," Lillian laughed.

"Well, you're right about that." Evelyn rolled her eyes.

"Hey, what's this? You women are ganging up on me," Harry protested.

"You asked for it, buddy," Walter snickered.

Ryan came over with Grace and sat down next to Walter and Lillian.

"Can everybody hear me?" he shouted. Walter jokingly put his hands to his ears. "Very funny, Walter," Ryan grinned.

"We can hear you, kid," Norman yelled from the middle of the pool.

"Okay, great. You guys know we're having a party in a few days for the end of our season. Grace and I would like to get a show of hands of how many of you plan on coming."

Everyone in the pool and the surrounding deck raised a hand.

"Wow. Oh, this is fantastic. Looks like we're gonna have a hell of a party. Grace started a list, and it's on the community bulletin board. We'd like to get some volunteers for food. I'm going to get a bunch of pizzas, and Grace is bringing a few cases of soda pop. We could use some help with maybe chips, water, paper products, and things like that. Oh, and we'll order a cake too."

Ryan pointed to the dry-erase board on the wall. "If you wouldn't mind thinking about it and then signing up before you leave, it would give us a better idea of what we might have to pick up last minute."

Grace interjected. "Thank you, everyone. I would like to say it has been so much fun spending time with all of you. We're definitely going to miss our morning crew." She smiled and blew out a kiss.

"She really is the sweetest," Walter whispered in Lillian's ear.

"They both are." Lillian smiled.

Walter stuck close to Lillian the entire day. He didn't know what he was waiting for, but if it happened, he'd be ready. Thankfully, the day passed without the need for heroics.

On the ride home, Lillian told Walter that she had decided to pick up some bakery cookies for the party. Though Ryan was getting a cake, some of the ladies loved the sweets from the Jewish bakery downtown.

Later in the evening, Walter approached Vivienne for a dish he could bring to the party. She made the best avocado pasta salad in the state. She happily agreed. Walter could rest easy knowing his contribution was solid.

Walter was going to stay the night, but Lillian insisted on some alone time. She needed to feel her independence again.

After dinner, he gave her a quick call to be sure she was doing all right. He had wanted to take her to dinner, but she wasn't up to it. He had almost suggested he'd get takeout and bring it over, but her exhaustion made him hold his tongue.

She told him dinner would be a can of soup and off to bed early.

His fear heightened when saying goodbye. Her voice trailed off, and there was silence. He shouted into the phone several times before he brought her back to the conversation. Reluctantly, he wished her a good night and sweet dreams. When he hung up the phone, the click gave him an eerie feeling of finality. The Lillian he knew was slipping away.

Vivienne and Robert had come in from the kitchen, where they each made a masterpiece hot fudge sundae. Robert had an extra bowl in his hand and set it down in front of Walter on a TV tray.

"Thank you." Walter scooped some whipped cream on the spoon. "Viv, how did you think Lillian looked today?"

"Exhausted."

"She's not her usual spunky self. For a while at the pool today, I saw a little of her old spirit, but it didn't last long. I'm not sure what to do."

"I don't think there is anything to be done. You said she stopped treatment. I think what's going on is the natural progression of the cancer. Spend time with her, give her room when she needs it, and be strong. She's going to need you."

Walter shook his head. It wasn't what he wanted to hear, but he knew in his heart that it was the truth.

"I think I'll go see Frank in the morning. Ryan said he agreed to an appearance or two at the center. We only have three days left. I want to be sure he actually makes it. If I can get him to drive, we can pick up Lillian on the way. If not, will you take us?"

"I can take you after my doctor's appointment at ten. I'll swing by and pick you up."

"I'll text you if Frank backs out." Walter assessed the empty bowl. "I think I'll have a little more."

Vivienne's glare said everything.

"I'm not an idiot. I'm only taking a spoon full."

That's when it started. The simple exchange of meaningless words that would escalate to the explosion of angry comebacks and guilt. Walter thought he had buried his negative emotions toward Vivienne, but he was wrong. Just one sharp look over the extra helping of ice cream set his blood boiling.

The kitchen light was off, and Walter flipped the switch on the wall. The air was thick with the lingering hot fudge that was heated in the microwave.

The aroma floated over and tickled his nostrils. He was only coming in for a spoonful of frozen delight, but now the yummy chocolaty ribbon of delectable liquid took its hold. Walter took two scoops of mint chip and piled on a heavy dose of fudge, whipped cream, and nuts.

Robert was still watching television, but Vivienne was not in the room. Her empty bowl sat on the coffee table. Walter sat in his recliner and placed the full bowl on the TV tray. Inching it toward him, he sealed himself into the direct path of the sugary heaven. Barely getting one spoonful into his watering mouth, he was abruptly interrupted by the pursed lips and shaking head of his daughter-in-law.

"What is wrong with you? Do you like letting your diabetes go through the roof?" Vivienne stood, arms crossed.

"That's my concern. And no, it won't. I'll take my injection later." Walter scooped another spoonful.

Vivienne huffed, "You've got to stop doing this, or else you'll be joining Mom."

Walter threw the spoon into the bowl. He abruptly pushed the TV tray away, causing the bowl to slide and plummet onto the carpet. Glancing down at the green and brown mess, he slammed his fist down on the billowy arm of the chair. Blurred vision fueled by an explosion igniting in his core, he stood up and deliberately stepped into the pile of mush. Gliding over the carpet with his shoes, he wiped them clean.

Walter wasn't done yet. Vivienne and Robert watched in horror as he hurled the TV tray across the room. It hit a corner of the curio sending a few of the frames plummeting to the plush carpet. Luckily, none of the glass shattered.

"What the hell is wrong with you?" Robert was holding his pregnant sobbing wife.

"I am sick and tired of being treated like a child. You had one. We lost him. I'm not his replacement. Neither is the one fermenting in her belly."

Walter heard the words echo throughout the room. He knew they were like the hot metal of bullets piercing their flesh and, yet, he couldn't stop.

"She's the reason he's dead. Her. It's all your fault my grandson is gone. All your fault we will never see him, hold him, hear his laughter ever again!"

"What in God's name are you talking about? Have you lost your mind? How is Vivienne responsible? It was a shooting. Some maniacal, frustrated idiot with a gun had a grudge. He killed our baby because he was sick. Where the fuck do you get off accusing his mother?" Robert shouted.

"Tell him," Walter screamed at Vivienne, "Tell him the whole truth!"

"What are you talking about? There's nothing for her to tell." Robert held Vivienne tighter.

"You know the truth. You know what you did and why the baby is gone. *Tell him why Chasey is not here today.* Just say it." Walter pressed his anger into the side of his chair.

Vivienne slithered down Robert's side and collapsed. Balled up with her knees to her chest, the tears flooded uncontrollably. Gasping for air, her body convulsed with each sob.

"He was my son! My son! Not a day, an hour—a minute— goes by that I don't play that morning over in my head. My baby is lost forever. Don't you think I'm well aware of what I did?"

Robert dropped to one knee and turned her over. He pulled her hands from her face and pushed the matted hair away from her face.

"What is my father ranting about?" Robert's voice quivered.

Vivienne blinked repeatedly before smearing the water from her eyes with her hands. The snotty liquid stuck to her upper lip, and Robert wiped it away with the sleeve of his shirt. He pulled her up and propped her limp body against the base of the couch. The shaking had stopped, and her breathing slowed.

Walter glared into the darkness of her blank stare. "Tell him," his words were sharp.

Vivienne turned to Robert. "He felt sick," her voice was small and trailing.

"What are you saying?" Robert sat next to her.

"That morning, when Chase got up, he felt a little nauseous. I wanted to keep him home, but he pleaded with me. He wanted to show off his war hero Grandpa to the class. I felt his head, and he was a little warm, so I took his temperature. It was barely 100 degrees.

"I insisted he stay home, but he cried so hard my heart broke. I let him go. I let my baby boy go to school that day, knowing I shouldn't. And he never came home. Walter's right. I am the reason our son is dead." Vivienne fell over onto Robert's shoulder.

Walter sat in his chair with the words resonating in his mind. The lifeless shell of a woman he had grown to love as a daughter was lying on the floor next to him. His rage was gone. The words crept into the depths of his belly and extinguished the flame that had been burning for the past eighteen months. But it wasn't an admission of guilt. The remarks left Vivienne and grazed Walter's ears. He realized for the first time that blaming her suddenly seemed absurd. If someone was truly to blame—it was him.

"It wasn't you. It was my fault. I failed him." Tears pooled in Walter's eyes.

Both Vivienne and Robert looked up.

"That day in the classroom, I was knocked down when the door flew open. He had the gun pointed at the kids, and they were crying. Chase was under his desk a few rows away from me. I knew he could slide to me quicker than I could get to him. I begged and pleaded for him to come to me, but he was too scared.

"The gunman spotted me and pointed the gun at my head, but Mr. Rutherford unexpectedly came in, and that's when he was shot in the chest. I tried to get up to get to him, but that bastard slammed the gun into the back of my head. Then he went crazy and started shooting. Everywhere. I blacked out after that.

"When I woke up, the shooter was gone, and the classroom was nothing but bodies and blood. Kids were crying and moaning. I crawled to each child, looking for Chasey. When I found him, he was face down. I turned him over, and I knew—I wasn't there for him. His *war hero* couldn't save him. His little face was so pale." Walter's wail carried through the room, filling it with indescribable pain.

"Dad." Robert's eyes were bloodshot and wet with tears. "You couldn't save him because a man with a gun penetrated the school. That's the only reason. No one could have known. Not a day goes by that I don't think of his happy little face. He had the best smile. But that asshole took him away. No one in this room." He reached out for Walter.

Walter turned away.

"Dad," Vivienne whispered. "We've kept secrets from each other for too long."

Walter swiveled around and faced them. He reached his hand out and grabbed hold of his son.

"I am so sorry, Viv. I've had so much anger. It was easier to blame you. But it was my guilt that has been consuming me. I hope you can forgive me?" Walter hunched over.

She reached out and clasped both of their hands with hers. Squeezing tightly, Vivienne fought back another round of tears.

"We all need to let go of the anger and guilt. We are all we have. If we give in, then that bastard just keeps winning. He will burn in hell for what he did that day, but my baby—our baby, he's safe. No one can ever hurt him again. And I know in my heart, we will see him again. Until that day comes, though, we need to live full lives. That is the only way to honor Chase."

Vivian rubbed her belly, and Robert stretched his fingers over hers. He eased her up, and they retreated to the second story.

Walter yearned to be with Lillian. She would hear his sins and talk him through the pain. It was getting late, but he had to see her. Deciding to go ask Vincent for a ride, he bundled up and hastened across the street. Hoping the face-to-face would give Vincent the incentive to go out in the elements of the brisk spring night, he hesitated before knocking. To Walter's delight, Vincent was drinking coffee and watching reruns of *NCIS*.

"Hey, come on in. What brings you out at this late hour?" Vincent sipped his coffee.

"Would you drive me to Lillian's?"

"Is everything okay? I mean, with Lillian?"

"Yes. She's fine. Just want to go over there." Walter checked his watch.

"I think *NCIS* can wait." Vincent grinned.

Walter nodded and smiled. He was relieved that his friend didn't pry too much. Going over the evening's events would be emotional enough when he got to Lillian's. Hashing it out twice would surely drain what little energy he had left. A sharp pain ripped through his center to his collarbone, and he quickly slammed his fist into the left side of his chest.

"You okay?"

"Yup. It's gone. Get a pain that comes around from time to time. I think Vivienne's making me eat too much health food. It's slowly killing me," Walter chuckled.

The two men chatted about politics and the price of gas before reaching Lillian's place. Walter got out and thanked his friend for the ride. As he watched Vincent drive away, he hoped Lillian wouldn't be too upset by the impromptu knock at her door.

When the door finally opened, Lillian was in her robe with sleep in her eyes. "Walter. What's wrong? Are you alright? Did something happen to Robert or Vivienne?"

"No. Everyone's fine." He shuffled his feet.

"Then why on earth are you standing on my porch at—I don't even know what time it is. It's late. It feels very late."

He froze. It all seemed so logical a half hour ago. But now, standing in the darkness, he felt like a fool.

"I'm sorry. I shouldn't have come. I'll call Vincent to come back."

"Nonsense. Get in here. It's freezing out there. Good thing it's spring. I swear the weather has been so unpredictable lately. Like someone I know."

Walter followed her into the kitchen, where she proceeded to put on a kettle of hot water. Not asking his preference, she set two cups with saucers and two bags of Earl Grey tea on the table. Beside it, she placed a small pitcher of cream and a glass bowl with sugar.

They waited at the table until the kettle sang. Lillian poured the steaming water into their cups, sat down, and added cream and sugar to hers. Walter followed her lead.

"Now, are you going to tell me what is going on, or shall I try to guess? Although you have already interrupted a lovely dream I was having about traveling to France, so I think it's best you spill the beans."

Walter hesitated and then cleared his throat. The emotions rising to the surface took hold and jolted him back to the confrontation earlier in the evening. His hands quivered as he struggled to push back the acid painting the back of his throat.

When the tale was complete, he closed his eyes and dropped his head. Rubbing his forehead, his skull pounded with the same melody of his heartbeat.

Lillian folded her hand into his. "I'm glad you came."

"I felt bad but good. Am I making sense?" Walter sniffled.

"Completely. It needed to happen, you know that, right?" Lillian caressed his cheek.

"I feel relieved, but at the same time hollow. Like everything has been drained from my body. Maybe a little ashamed."

"Ashamed? Why?"

"Vivienne. And Robert, too. I have been completely miserable to them. Especially her. How they have put up with me all this time is mind-boggling."

"They love you. No one knows as much as they do the pain you are going through."

Walter gazed out the window into the darkness. "I know you're right. I wish I could change everything."

"Ah. But you can't. The only thing any one of us can do is to move forward."

"What about you? Do you think stopping your treatment is moving forward?" Walter played with the teacup.

"I do. You know how sick the chemo was making me. My life was slowly being robbed of all the things that make me—me. I am nearly ninety-two years old, and I've had a hell of a journey. I don't want to end it withered in pain because I'm too nauseous to move. I'm choosing to move forward and get on with it. I'm at peace with my decision. I want to enjoy every drop of every day while I'm still able to.

"You know we don't only make memories for ourselves," she continued. "Everything we do in our lives ripples into the thoughts of those around us. We'll make new memories that will live on in our friends, our family, and those lives we touch every day. That's moving forward."

Walter loved her eyes. They were so calm. Her words wrapped around him and sweetened the bitterness that had once been his soul. He finally got it. The arguing and yelling drained him and released the shame and guilt. But Lillian, she lit the candle to shine his way out of the darkness.

They finished their tea and then went upstairs to the bedroom. He held her close through the night until the first beam of sunshine pierced the glass and rested at the foot of the bed. It was a new day.

Chapter Eighteen

There was one day left before the big bash to usher in the summer schedule and the end of the senior program. Walter and Lillian remained busy the entire day coordinating food and decorations with Ryan and Grace.

Lillian drove to the bakery with Walter. The lure of Italian cookies and pastries could bring her out even on a not-so-good day. Vincent had convinced Frank to attend the party, even though he hadn't gone to the pool since Elsa's death. His argument, he told Walter, was that if Lillian could attend and everyone could see she wasn't at her best, then so could Frank.

At first, Walter was not too happy with Vincent's course of persuasion, but then Lillian said if it got Frank out of the house, then she didn't mind. He needed to be with his friends.

When the to-do list was completed, Lillian parked in front of Walter's house and kissed him. She told him he should spend the evening with his family, and he agreed. It was time to move forward.

Walter walked through the front door to the glorious smell of homemade pot roast, carrots, and potatoes. The scent caught his nostrils and carried him into the kitchen, where Viv was stirring a pot of brown gravy. None of that packet stuff either. She always made hers from scratch.

"This house smells delicious," he proclaimed.

Vivienne spun around and smiled. "Dinner's ready in ten minutes."

Stacking three plates, napkins, and silverware, he set them down on the dining room table.

Robert breezed through the room just when the last knife was set down.

"What? No television with dinner tonight?'

"I think tonight we should eat at the dining room table if that's alright?' Walter straightened a plate.

"Actually, I think that's a great idea." Robert patted his father's shoulder.

Conversation took second place to the culinary delight. Walter hadn't enjoyed a meal as much as this in a very long time. He savored every bite. Vivienne's laughter filled him with a hope he hadn't allowed himself to feel in years. She and Robert were vibrant and glowing with the energy of life they created, and she caressed her belly.

He eagerly listened as they exchanged stories about their day, appreciating the beauty in the simplistic ritual of dinner at the dining room table.

That night before closing his eyes, he said a prayer for the first time since Gina had passed away. He thanked the heavens for all the good in his life and then added an extra plea for Frank and Lillian. He wanted them both to enjoy the party tomorrow and leave behind, if only for the day, any pain holding them hostage. It would be a good day; he felt it in his bones.

As the sun rose, drenching Walter's skin with life, he took in the excitement of new possibilities. Sitting up, he was captivated by the kaleidoscope dancing around the room and gracing the walls with ribbons of yellow and orange. He never realized how much he liked this room. Glancing at his bride in their wedding photo hanging above the bureau, he felt the comfort of home.

This was his space. His things, his sanctuary. He smiled as he made the morning trek to the bathroom.

A warm shower, combing of the hair, and a splash of aftershave, and he was ready. He chose a button-up shirt to go with black slacks and oxfords. Briefly contemplating a tie, he decided against it. He wanted to be presentable for Lillian, not look like he was dressed for the prom. Vincent arrived at ten o'clock sharp. They would pick up Lillian on the way. Ryan had asked if they could get there a little early to help with the decorations. Lillian couldn't wait to get started. She loved decorating. It was fun creating the once plain into something magical.

She was waiting outside by the curb, balancing two pink boxes. The pastries and cookies filled the car with scents of vanilla, almond, and chocolate. Walter couldn't wait to attack them.

"Those smell yum," Walter proclaimed.

Lillian shut the car door and buckled up. "You're not getting any of them until they have been properly set up at the food table."

"Not even one cookie? No one will know."

"I will know." Lillian gripped both boxes.

Walter didn't stand a chance, so he dropped it. He would just have to be the first in line to get his pick.

Ryan and Grace greeted them at the door of the Center with huge smiles and a good morning. They draped tablecloths on the folding tables that Ryan had supplied, and Lillian helped Grace with the decorations.

Before long, everyone else started to trickle in. When Walter saw Frank, he grinned. After refusing their offer for a ride, he secretly thought Frank wouldn't show. But there he was. Frank immediately headed straight for Lillian. She glanced over at Walter and winked.

After stealing a cookie when Lillian was distracted, Walter sat down and soaked in the festivities. All his friends had showed, and others he hadn't seen in quite some time. In fact, it was like the town's senior group reunion. Norman, Adolfo, Harry, and Evelyn clustered around a table, with Lillian and Frank at the center of the mix. Vincent had taken a seat next to Mary Murdoch, and, from what little Walter could hear, he was angling for a date later.

There must be sixty people here, Walter thought. "Great turn out, kid. You two really did a good job," Walter shouted to Ryan.

"Thanks. We're pretty happy with the turnout." Ryan flashed a toothy grin.

"Hey, Mr. Riley, what are you doing over here by yourself?" Lillian sat beside Walter.

"I was taking it all in. You know, I can't remember when we were all together like this. I'm seeing folks here that haven't been around in a long time. It's good to see everybody enjoying themselves."

"I know what you mean." Lillian lay her head back on the chair. "They're all happy. This day is just perfect."

Walter leaned over and kissed her cheek. "It sure is."

The party lasted longer than anyone had anticipated. With plenty of food, conversation, and nowhere special to be, everyone lingered until the shadows indicated the close of the day.

Almost everyone stayed to help clean up. By the time the last table was folded, no one would have ever known a party had taken place. Walter and Lillian gave out plenty of hugs and promises to keep in touch before piling their weary bodies into Vincent's car. Frank followed behind them before turning off to stop at the market on the way home.

"I hope Frank is feeling better." Vincent broke the quiet.

"I think he'll be fine," Lillian chimed.

"Why do you say that?" Walter asked.

"He said he'll help me when I need it; just call him."

"That is a good sign," Walter agreed.

When they reached Lillian's house, Walter got out and walked her to the door.

"Thank you," he whispered.

"For what?"

"For showing me how to live again."

He grabbed her by the waist and eased her closer to him. Gently his lips cascaded across hers. He moved to her neck and then cheek before one last taste. Walter waited until she was inside and heard the deadbolt lock before joining Vincent in the car. Once again, his friend was a gentleman and never mentioned a word of their goodnight exchange.

"Today was great. I got a date with Mary Murdoch next Saturday night. I'm not sure where we should go, though." Vincent glanced at Walter.

"Why don't you take her to Santucci's? You can never go wrong with Italian."

"Hmm. I like that. Santucci's it is. Would you like to go to breakfast in the morning? I was thinking maybe we could get Frank to go." Vincent pulled into the driveway.

"Sounds good. You gonna call him?" Walter opened the door.

"Yeah. I'll try in the morning. Is eight good for you?"

"That works."

"Either way, I'll see you then."

Walter slammed the door shut and waved over his shoulder as he walked across the street to home. The lights were on and, in the night's blanket of darkness, it warmed the way.

Robert and Vivienne were putting their coats on as he walked into the entryway.

"Where are you two headed off to?"

"We have a dinner reservation at Santucci's." Robert helped Vivienne with her coat.

Walter chuckled.

"What's so funny?" Robert dangled his keys.

"Nothing."

"How was the party? We thought for sure you'd be home earlier. It must have been nice."

"It was. We had so many people show up."

"That's great. There's leftover pot roast in the refrigerator if you get hungry later." Vivienne hugged him.

"Thank you." Walter smiled. "I'm kind of full, but I'm sure I can make room for some of your pot roast a little later."

Vivienne laughed, and she and Robert said their goodbyes before closing and locking the door.

Walter went up to his room and changed into his pajamas. It was a great day, but he was beat. After he folded his pants and hung up his shirt, he retreated to the bathroom to clean his teeth. Placing the paste on his brush he felt a twinge of pain radiate up his left arm and seize hold of his shoulder. He dropped his toothbrush in the sink as he clutched the counter with one hand and his chest with the other. Perspiration rose to the surface of his skin and across his forehead as he struggled with the pain.

But as quickly as it had gripped him, its release was equally as fast. In moments, his breathing returned to normal, and he relaxed.

Walter sat down on the edge of the tub, assessing the episode. He guessed it was probably a muscle spasm brought on by moving the heavy tables around earlier that day. He stood up carefully and splashed a few handfuls of cold water on his face. It felt soothing. Promising himself he would take it easy for the next few days, he ambled downstairs and put on his favorite lineup of reruns. *Criminal Minds,* followed by *Blue Bloods,* and then, capping off the evening, *Murder She Wrote.*

After the FBI successfully solved a slew of serial murders, he found himself getting a rumble in his belly. Pot roast. The best kind of cure for hunger pangs.

Fixing a large dish, he popped it in the microwave, carried the plate into the living room, and placed it on the newly mended TV tray. The pot roast was even better reheated. Walter slopped up the gravy-drenched meal with a large dinner roll he had found on the counter in a plastic bag. Vivienne must have picked them up at the store earlier that day. If they had been there last night, he would have surely eaten at least one.

When he was finished, his sweet tooth called, and he decided to answer with a small ice cream sundae. He checked the clock and noticed he had only a minute or two left of *Blue Bloods*. He loaded his dirty dishes in the dishwasher instead. It didn't matter. The crime was already solved. He didn't need to hear the life lesson delivered by Tom Selleck. He already had enough of his own.

Making it just in time for the opening scene of *Murder She Wrote*, Walter reclined his chair and settled in for Jessica Fletcher's perfect record of catching the killer. But this time, he didn't catch her sleuthing.

When he opened his eyes again, the news was on. *Damn.* He got up and peeked out the front window. The car wasn't in the driveway. Robert and Vivienne were not home yet. He turned off the television and left the living room light on so they wouldn't walk into a dark house. He glanced at Chase's Disney picture and then picked it up and kissed it before taking his weary body up the fourteen steps.

He ambled into his bedroom and flipped on the light. It was a bit stuffy. Unlocking the top of his window, he pushed it up, leaving about a six-inch gap. The cool breeze crept in, and he shivered before turning down the covers. Turning off the light, Walter let the streetlamp and the moonlight guide his way to bed. Sitting on the edge of the mattress, his thoughts traveled to Lillian's porch and the goodnight kiss they had shared earlier. Her lips were always so soft. Once again, the twinge. A breath-halting pain burned its way briefly through his arm and then calmed itself.

Walter lay down and pulled the comforter up to his neck. There was nothing like a crisp night spent under a layer of warm covers. Closing his eyes, he allowed sleep to take over and whisk him away.

He didn't feel the slowing of his heart or the tightness in his chest. His thoughts traveled to a vision of stars shining in a vast space. His body, weightless like the air surrounding him, floated closer to the twinkle of lights cascading over the dark sky. Turning toward the earth, his house grew smaller with each passing moment. He felt no fear. A tunnel of warm light pierced a hole in the darkness. Walter reached out. Inching closer to the brilliant glow, he squinted to get a clearer view of the small shadow moving toward him; he hesitated for a moment.

"Chasey?" Walter gasped.

"Grandpa!"

THE END

239 Saving a Life

About the Author

Originally from New York, I currently reside in Nevada. Writing Young Adult paranormal, I find my inspiration from events that have been in my life for as long as I can remember.

Inheriting my sensitivity to the supernatural from my family, they continue to be an endless source of vision.

www.vickiannbush.com

241 Saving a Life

Also by Vicki-Ann Bush

Alex McKenna Series

Alex McKenna and the Geranium Deaths

Alex McKenna & The Geranium Deaths – Audible Edition

Alex McKenna & The Academy of Souls – Audible Edition

Alex McKenna & A Winter's Night - Audible Edition

Stand-alone titles

Ophelia

The Garden of Two

Saving A Life

The Queen of IT

Winslow Willow the Woodland Fairy

Short Stories

The Joshua Tree

Surviving

COMING 2024

The Darkest Light - YA Paranormal Romance - A teen angel, a tormented demon, and a bond that can't be broken

Liminal Space - Sci-Fi

www.ingramcontent.com/pod-product-compliance
Lightning Source LLC
LaVergne TN
LVHW041540070426
835507LV00011B/848